C000120446

WALKING BACKWARDS

WALKING BACKWARDS

Dealing with Guilt

Jeff Lucas

Authentic

Copyright © 2010 Jeff Lucas

First published by Scripture Union 1977, reprinted 1998

16 15 14 13 12 11 10 7 6 5 4 3 2 1

This edition first published 2010 by Authentic Media Limited
Milton Keynes
www.authenticmedia.co.uk

The right of Jeff Lucas to be identified as the Author of this Work has been
asserted by him in accordance with the Copyright, Designs and Patents Act 1988.

All rights reserved. No part of this publication may be reproduced,
stored in a retrieval system, or transmitted in any form or
by any means, electronic, mechanical, photocopying, recording or
otherwise, without the prior permission of the publisher or a licence
permitting restricted copying. In the UK such licences are issued by the
Copyright Licensing Agency, 90 Tottenham Court Road, London, W1P 9HE

British Library Cataloguing in Publication Data
A catalogue record for this book is available from the British
Library

ISBN: 978-1-85078-854-6

Unless otherwise stated, Scripture is taken from the Holy Bible, New
International Version. Copyright © 1973, 1978, 1984 by International Bible
Society. Anglicisation copyright © 1979, 1984, 1989. Used by permission of
Hodder and Stoughton Ltd.

Cover design Moose77
Printed in Great Britain by J.F. Print, Sparkford

Dedicated to the memory of my father, Stanley Lucas, 1920–1995

Most Christians have enough religion to feel guilty
about their sins,
but not enough to enjoy life in the Spirit.
Martin Luther

Contents

Chapter 1

The awkward art of walking backwards

Most folks, it seems, are better acquainted with their guilt and shame than with their God.

Charles Swindoll

'Skegness is s-ooo very bracing!' the holiday poster chortled.

Above the caption a rather overweight and jolly cartoon character, dressed in a 1930s bathing suit, danced on the golden sands of Skegness beach, ecstatic with joy that a force-twelve gale was threatening to tear his black-and-white striped swimsuit off.

'Skegness is s-ooo very like an armpit,' I muttered to no one in particular as I strolled along the pebble-dashed beach in the driving rain. Golden sand seemed to be in short supply; crude concrete steps marched down to yellow-foamed stones and rotting piles of stranded seaweed. Only an hour ago the walk had seemed a wonderful idea. It was raining hard enough to make Noah nervous, and the wind was whipping brown-stained waves into a polluted frenzy. But I was due to speak that night at Spring Harvest. There was too much going on in my chalet – hardly a peaceful atmosphere for careful spiritual preparation. Besides, after being at Spring Harvest for eight days I was feeling the need to get away for a while: I was starting to wake up in the middle of the night screaming 'Shine, Jesus, shine' at the top of my voice . . . So I decided to brave the deluge. I felt strangely invincible as I donned my trusty green wax coat – determined, challenged even, to walk the coastline alone.

The security man gave me a pass and a look that said, 'You don't need a coat, pal, you need a straitjacket.' He was right. The first forty-five minutes presented no difficulties as I walked with the wind at my back, thinking and praying and enjoying the deserted promenade. But the weather was conspiring with the sea, lulling me into a false sense of security.

When I decided to turn round and head back to camp, my problems began. In a moment, everything changed. The wind was now punching me in the face, a solid smack with each new gust, sharpening the downpour into millions of freezing needles that pricked and numbed my cheeks. I put my head down and stumbled on but in seconds I was totally soaked, half blind and very, very cold. My jeans clung skin-tight to numb legs. There seemed to be only one solution: to turn round and walk home – backwards. Quickly I looked along the promenade, just to make sure that no other escaped lunatics from Butlins were on hand to witness an adult marching backwards along the beach. Feeling very silly indeed, I began the long trek in reverse.

At first it felt fine, a relief even, as the wind battered my back rather than my face. But I only managed a few yards. God hadn't granted me the gift of reverse gear. I was swerving all over the place. It was awkward and uncomfortable. I felt I was going to fall at any moment. After about three minutes, I gave up and turned to face the turbo-charged rain again. It felt like I was lifting my head to the force of an ice-cold power shower, but at least I was heading in the right direction. Despite the weather, to turn round and face the front again was a relief.

It is exhausting, confusing and awkward to walk backwards. For me, a couple of minutes in reverse was more than enough. But many people spend great chunks of their lives 'walking backwards', figuratively speaking, and their uncomfortable march is more like an interminable marathon than just one wasted, wet afternoon.

How do we get caught up in such exhausting and fruitless activity? It often begins when we commit some sin, large or small – if indeed sin can be measured – and then refuse fully to accept God's forgiveness. We try to move on, but find it almost impossible to forget that dark moment of failure. We are paralysed with guilt. We don't *feel* forgiven. Though we may have a good evangelical theology of grace, what we actually experience are condemnation and guilt.

Sometimes we walk backwards as a result of being sinned against. If you are the victim of physical, sexual or spiritual abuse, you may live with an unexplained sense of shame. Or perhaps you have struggled for years with negative feelings about your sexuality, your motives, your pride, your jealousy – maybe you even feel guilty about feeling guilty. Or perhaps you feel guilty for no reason apparent to you at all.

I know what I'm talking about. I spent a long time in reverse gear, constantly looking over my shoulder at an assortment of past sins. I loved God, desperately wanted to please him – and wasted seven long years walking backwards. And I have discovered that there are thousands of other Christians who have been fellow backward-hikers. There are huge battalions of God's soldiers staggering across the battlefield in reverse. Perhaps you are one of them.

Maybe, like me, the long march backwards began when you were relatively young in the faith. Remember those heady, naive days when all Christians seemed bionically super-holy? How long did it take you to work out that you might just have to learn to deal with failure? My infant Christian heart understood all too well what the word 'sin' meant, but I didn't have such a clear definition of that other word, 'forgiveness'. The day came when I made what I considered to be quite a serious mistake. Looking back on it now, I shouldn't have made such a big deal out of it.

There are a lot of 'should haves'. I should have asked God to forgive me, and believed and accepted that he had, there and then. I should have known that inner feelings of guilt and shame aren't infallible signposts to correct conclusions. I should have shared my private struggles with a mature Christian friend and thus brought them out into the open. Perhaps someone could have told me that new Christians often have especially tender consciences and every single twinge of guilt isn't necessarily from God.

However, though I dropped the sin, I ended up holding on to the memory of it for years. In fact the memory was so vivid, it seemed as if a video recorder was replaying it over and over again inside my head. Stop. Rewind. Play. Stop. Rewind. Play. Every time the memory came, I would set out on the same long mental journey which would only end as I assured myself that I really was forgiven, that God would surely not torture me with my past. But relief was only temporary. Soon some trigger would slam me back into replay mode, and I would start

4

on the same old trek again. I sobbed my way through countless services and almost lost all hope. I would put my head down and cover my ears to block out the sounds of prayers or songs so that I could concentrate wholly on my personal mind trip.

Perhaps you are doing the same. Perhaps when you try to read the Bible, your mistake comes into your mind in vivid Technicolor. Perhaps when the preacher thunders stirring words of challenge, you blush with guilt and shame. Perhaps, like me, you 'repent' repeatedly.

The worst thing was, I couldn't help but believe that God himself was punching the remote control of this inner mental video player, that he was angry with me because of what I had done and was reminding me as part of some elaborate punishment programme. When I prayed, I tried to call him 'Father', but it sounded hollow. Finding the will of God for the future became impossible, I was so preoccupied with looking over my shoulder at my past. My feelings of guilt were deep, almost physical, compulsive.

I would like to say that one wonderful day I woke up to find light pouring in through the ceiling and a shimmering angel standing at my bedside, screaming *'Don't be daft, Jeffrey, you're forgiven!'* The truth is that the sense of freedom came gradually. After years of walking backwards, it slowly began to dawn on me that I didn't have to suffer any more. I learned that it was God's will for me to turn round, face the future and leave the past finally and completely behind. I learned that there was indeed a finger on that remote control button which seemed to taunt me, but it wasn't the finger of God. It was my own hand of pride as I stoically refused to lean hard on God's kindness. It was the Pharisaic finger of negative religion – manipulation in the name of God thrives among the guilt-ridden. And sometimes it was

5

the gnarled finger of the denizen of a lower world – if not Satan, then at least one of his harassing agents. But it wasn't the good hand of God. What a wonderful relief, to face the present and the future again with joy and hope!

Are you walking backwards right now? Is there something you did back in the dim and distant past: you have turned from it, repented of it, but you can't forget it? Are you watching private showings of your yesterdays that torment you? If you are, then please read *all* I have to say in these next few pages. I don't approach this subject of guilt as a psychologist, and I am aware that there will be some readers who will need to seek professional help, so deep and compulsive is their problem with guilt and shame. Rather, I come to the subject as someone with a deep love for Scripture and the Church, the community of God.

I am aware, too, of the limitations of a slim volume such as this: it cannot begin to offer definitive answers to the questions that such a complex subject will raise. But I do hope you will laugh, cry and learn with me as we begin to explore together. This is an investigation God wants us to make. He paints a portrait of guilt early on in his word. The opening chapters of the Bible draw back the curtain on the original couple, Adam and Eve, covered in shame, fleeing from him in paradise. My prayer is that the God of outrageous, wonderful grace will gently break through the layers of your guilt, however long you have lived with them. It is time to allow him to erase those mental video tapes once and for all. It is time to let him love you.

Walking backwards – it's tiresome, painful and unnatural. And if you're a Christian, it's not for you.

Chapter 2

The burden of false guilt

Shame is a very heavy feeling . . . like a hunk of lead on our hearts.

Lewis Smedes

'Almost done,' the doctor smiled, scribbling furiously on a clipboard. I tried in vain to read his upside-down scrawl, but it was quite unintelligible. My friendly physician had managed to complete eight years of postgraduate education, but like most medical types, the poor chap had never learned how to write. I scanned the page again, hoping to glean some idea of my projected life expectancy, but to no avail. Apparently a demented fly had dipped himself in blue ink and done the salsa all over the page.

I hate medical examinations. Who in their right mind wants to stand stripped in the presence of someone fully clothed, be pushed, pulled, prodded, hit with a rubber hammer on the shin and made to cough to order, all the time wondering if your underwear is in fashion/clean/without holes?

'Time for a quick X-Ray then,' said my torturer brightly. I wrapped myself in a towelling dressing gown and trudged down the corridor to a room with a sign on the door: 'X-Ray, Danger!' This, together with a yellow-and-black nuclear symbol made me feel all warm and welcome. The radiologist was waiting for me, but was also in need of her regular fix of caffeine, so her greeting was brief. I looked round the room. An X-Ray machine, a medical couch and, on the couch, an apron made of lead which, I later discovered, weighed about thirty pounds.

'I'm off for a quick coffee break, back in a minute,' said the radiologist. Then, as she stepped out of the door, she pointed at the mysterious lead apron and I *thought* she said, 'Put that round your neck.'

Of course, now I know she said no such thing. Blessed with brilliant hindsight, I now realise, thank you very much, that the lead apron weighing thirty pounds belonged round my *waist*. But at the time, reason and intelligence sent packing by embarrassment and confusion, I thought that Florence 'Nescafe' Nightingale had told me to tie it round my neck.

So I did what I thought I was told. I grabbed the heavy apron with both hands and hauled it awkwardly up onto my chest. So far, so good. It seemed to weigh a ton and was extremely uncomfortable, but mine was not to reason why.

Now I just had to tie it on. A three-foot length of webbing appeared from each side of the apron. Holding the lead with one hand so that it didn't fall off my chest and break my toes (thus creating the need for another X-Ray), I took one of the tapes and threw it around my neck, then repeated the process on the other side. I completed the procedure by tying a very large bow.

Flushed with success, I tried to stand upright – and immediately felt unwell. Something must be wrong. The weight threatened to push me backwards onto the floor.

It was impossible to lean forward: the pressure was too great on my neck. I couldn't move.

I began to sweat.

I began to pray that the radiologist would come back quickly and rescue me.

I began to pray that Jesus would come back quickly and rescue me.

I began to think uncharitable thoughts about Sir Walter Raleigh or whoever it was who discovered coffee and so was the indirect inventor of coffee breaks.

I stood there for about twenty years (five minutes actually, but you know what I mean) until the caffeine-charged radiologist returned. As she walked into the room and caught sight of me, her face immediately declared war on itself. She obviously wanted to slap her thighs, throw her head back and laugh for half an hour. But she was a professional. With supreme effort, she locked her facial muscles, looked at me and simply said, 'No . . .'

Take a mental snapshot of me standing there, a reasonably intelligent adult male, totally immobilised by lead. Forgive me for mixing my metaphors, but it's a useful illustration of what a life lived with guilt looks like – not only do you walk backwards, as we saw in chapter 1, but you stagger around with a ton-weight wrapped round your neck.

When Jesus wanted to show what negative religion and the guilt it creates feel like, he painted a picture using the analogy of a heavy weight: 'You experts in the law, woe to you, because you load people down with burdens they can hardly carry, and you yourselves will not lift one finger to help them' (Luke 11:46).

At the heart of the gospel of Christ is an invitation to unload this excess baggage and not to pick up more tonnage. Hear Jesus again: 'Come to me, all you who are weary and burdened, and I will give you rest. Take my yoke upon you and learn from me, for I am gentle and humble in heart, and you will find rest for your souls. For my yoke is easy and my burden is light' (Matt. 11:28–30).

The picture Jesus paints is that of someone staggering along the road of life, impossibly weighed down, worn out and weary as a result. His words are more than just colourful 'preacher talk' – false guilt can and will seriously damage your health. Shame is a very heavy feeling. It is a feeling that we do not measure up and maybe will never measure up to the sort of people we are meant to be. The feeling, when we are conscious of it, gives us a vague disgust with ourselves, which in turn feels like a hunk of lead on our hearts.[1]

The distortion of our own image

Unhealthy shame spills over everything we are . . . it flops, sloshes, and smears our whole being . . .[2]

When you walk backwards carrying the burden of guilt, your eyes are on the floor and you can't see where you're going (obviously!). You can't see past successes and victories, the high points of your life. Only your failures, real or imagined – the low points – are in view. The quiet, daily work of the Holy Spirit, who weaves strands of goodness and godliness in you, goes unnoticed. You can't see the guiding hand of God leading you on. You may be growing, but you don't know it. You don't have a true picture of the future hope God has planned for you, and you are unable to appreciate truly the gifts and abilities he has given you.

A story is told of the great Michelangelo, the master artist who captured so much of the potent colour and power of Creation Day on the ceiling of the Sistine Chapel. After a particularly difficult day up on the back-breaking scaffolding, the great man wrote these words in his journal: 'I am not a painter.'

Millions have stood beneath that breathtaking canopy, witnesses all to the utter absurdity of his self-verdict. But temporary failure had blinded him. The genius who could 'see' the birth of the cosmos in his mind, and capture that glory with his brush and paint, lost sight of himself. Fortunately, his blindness was momentary. Michelangelo soon shook the scales from his eyes and went on to complete one of the most magnificent works in the history of art. He *was* a painter.

Often those of us who are feeling chronically guilty take much longer to recover. Focusing back on a fleeting moment of weakness, we begin to build our identity around that shadowy incident. This is a subtle but critical step. Instead of feeling that our *sin* was wrong – as indeed it was – we may begin to feel that we ourselves are wrong. Instead of feeling moral pain about *what we did*, we begin to agonise about *who we are*. But we judge ourselves falsely. Many years ago, one of my children taught me that lesson.

The child in question, quite out of character, decided to conceal some information about a planned trip from me, thinking that I might say 'No' if I knew the full details. I was deceived, so in a sense I was told a lie. When the truth came out, I wrongly suggested that my child was a liar. With a few cutting words, I tried to identify an entire character according to those dishonourable few seconds. Quickly the answer came back: 'No, Daddy, I am not a liar. I just told a lie this time – and I'm sorry.' At first I was tempted to dismiss this argument out of hand as an attempt to play games with words, a bid to wriggle out of the issue. Then I remembered something I had read a few days earlier

> Some people tell one lie, and in the twinkling of an eye, they are liars . . . they go to a party, talk too much, tell a story to the left of good taste, are reminded of it on the way home, and sink into a funky shame for being half witted fools. This makes about the same sense as saying that if you pound a nail in a piece of wood you become a carpenter . . .[3]

Psychology professor Lewis Smedes recounts a true story as a tragic illustration

There was once in the city of Karpov, it is said, a gifted piano player named Lech Koplenski who, because he had no connections in the concert world, played the piano every night at a popular cabaret. Chenska Wolenka was an attractive woman who loved Lech, with a selfless devotion to his dream of becoming a concert pianist. A producer of concerts often came to the cabaret, and Chenska struck up a friendship with him so that she could bring Lech to his attention.

The producer of concerts made Chenska a proposition. If she would make love with him, he would see to it that Lech got his chance on the concert stage. She agreed, and in his bed she made good on her bargain. The producer made good on his as well. Lech did indeed play the piano on the concert stage.

Lech went off on concert tours, became a star, and did not come back to the cabaret. All that Chenska had left over was a deep shame of herself. One early morning in May she jumped from her apartment window to her death in a Karpov alley. Taped to her mirror was this sentence: *I am filth.*[4]

One unclean act. Selfless, pure motives led her to impurity, but that single compromise taunted, jeered and clamoured for Chenska's attention, finally convincing her that she was scum. And she martyred herself for a false cause. She died for a lie. Take it from me, guilt can be a burden that can and will crush the life out of us.

John Quincy Adams was also struck by this self-blindness. He saw himself as the proverbial worm, complaining, 'My life has been spent in vain and idle aspirations, and in ceaseless rejected prayers that something beneficial should be the result of my existence.' From his words you would think he did nothing with his life. Actually, he served as Ambassador to Holland, Ambassador to Great Britain, Ambassador to Russia, Secretary of State, Senator and President of the United States. Yet guilt managed to shout louder than his heady list of accomplishments and branded him useless.

The distortion of God's image

False guilt disguises God and dresses him up as a Pharisee rather than a father. It robs us of the beauty of the most beautiful, turning God instead into a monster who mocks us by calling himself 'Abba.' As we are swept along by the wave of confusion, false guilt claims an authority over us that is utterly intimidating. The thought that God himself might be the prosecuting attorney is terrifying.

To lose sight of the true God is a problem that will affect more than your theology. It has been said that 'What we think about God determines how we live.' It's true. People who think God is miserable, antiseptic and passionless tend to end up acting and looking like their imagined God. People who serve a God who complains and criticises them day and night aren't too easy to live with, as they become 'Godlike' themselves.

It didn't take me long as a new Christian to develop a feeling that God was never really quite pleased with me, I could quote endless Scriptures about his love, but inwardly remained unconvinced that he actually *liked* me. I knew he was the Creator of joy, but felt nervous about laughter and fun. What gave me these ideas? I don't really know. Perhaps the preacher of a particularly disturbing sermon. Perhaps a Christian movie that spelt out in horrifying terms what it would be like to be left behind after Jesus had come back. Perhaps the advice of the person who told me that God's will for my life was probably going to be the exact opposite of anything I might enjoy! Whatever the reason, I ended up with a frowning, killjoy God who would never allow me to bask in the sunshine of his approval, no matter how much I longed to. It got so bad, I ended up kneeling one day to apologise to my God for the fact that I felt happy. Guilt had drawn a curtain and hidden the real God from view.

Sounds strange? I've met thousands of Christians who compulsively count themselves *in* when the preacher is shouting loudly about sin and judgement – then count themselves *out* when he or she speaks softly about God's love and grace and kindness. This principle was dramatically acted out before my eyes some years ago when I was speaking at a youth camp on the beautiful Isle of Wight. I was preaching about relationships in general and gossip in particular, and felt the need to grab everyone's attention. I stood up and made a brief, simple announcement which had much the same effect as dropping a bomb: 'Ladies and gentlemen, there is a member here who has been causing a great deal of trouble and distress. People have been hurt and seriously wounded by you; people have left the church because of you. Tonight, in a few moments, I will publicly name you, the member who has caused this terrible damage.'

As you can imagine, the place went quiet. Deathly quiet. Blood drained from people's faces. They gripped the chairs in front of them with whitened knuckles. My intention was not to cause pain in some mindlessly sadistic fashion – rather, there was an important truth to communicate and the tension was all part of the lesson. I built up the atmosphere in the tent until it seemed that cardiac arrests on a large scale were inevitable. The piano player, who had looked perfectly happy before I started, actually got down and hid behind the piano, so terrified was he.

For about five torturous minutes I railed and yelled about the evils of this said member. Then, feeling that my audience were about to rush out of the tent and collectively throw themselves over the nearby cliffs, I decided to make my announcement: 'The name of this member, which has caused so much trouble here, is . . . the tongue, which the Authorised Version of the Bible says "is an unruly member" . . .'

People gasped. Sweat dripped. And the relief set in. Vice-like knuckles uncurled from metal chair-frames. Desperate brows that had been heavily furrowed smoothed themselves out. There was a resurrection at the piano as our maestro popped up smiling again and took his place at the keys.

However, it was after this meeting that I learned something about human nature. I had a line of people who came to tell me that they were convinced I was going to name *them*.

I quizzed them all. Were they harbouring secret evils and torrid sins in their hearts? Were they on the run from God and jumpy that they were about to feel his hand on their collars? The answer in every case was negative. These trembling fugitives were all Christians who were living for God to the best of their ability. They just had this terrible expectation that their names would be called in the event of any judgement roll-call. One writer describes this feeling: 'I lug around inside of me a dead weight of not-good-enoughness.'

When we feel this way, we don't even need to sin in order to trigger our guilt. We just sense that we are mediocre, not up to standard, all the time – like the gate-crashers rather than the guests at God's party, those who don't really belong. Every pastor and evangelist knows that there are some people who rush to the front every time an 'altar call' is given. The call may be for repentance, fresh commitment to prayer, or something else. But the same people respond every time. Why? I think it is because they have an inbuilt expectation of guilt and judgement. Catholic priests used to refer to people like these as 'the scrupulous' – those who hold on tight to guilt and are unable to accept grace.

Of course, for all those who rush forward, there are others who will not venture to make any public act of repentance because they are so paralysed by shame and hopelessness. They just sit in silence and suffer. And don't think for a moment that their guilt actually produces any fruit for good – the reverse is true. Demotivated and fearful, these people tend to sit on the fringes of their Christian life, unable to grow in character or grace. They are so busy

chasing phantoms from their yesterdays that there is neither time nor energy to consider the real issues of today, or
move forward into the hope of tomorrow.

The destruction of our joy

*Guilt . . . a knife cutting deep into the heart of me just when
I am feeling good about myself.*

Anon

It was our wedding day. The sun shone, my bride was
beautiful, and friends and family had gathered to celebrate with us. Yet, as I look back on that day, now nearly
thirty years ago, I have to confess that there was an unre-
lenting feeling of guilt gnawing away at my joy. Once
again, this guilt was illogical: it centred around the fact
that I was marrying the woman I loved deeply, but I felt
it was too good to be true. How could God be allowing
me to be so blessed? I smiled as the camera flash bulbs
popped, but deep down inside I wondered – was God
smiling? Guilt spoiled the day. How about your 'perfect
days'? You know the feeling. The world is your oyster, at
least for a little while. The bright summer sun warms
your back but doesn't burn you. An evening spent with
cherished friends leaves you feeling pleasantly tired but
glad to be alive. You are happy enough to laugh out loud,
even though no one has told a joke. The presence of God
is so poignant, a breathless but joyful hush settles over
you . . . Then past memories flow back in, bringing guilt
in their wake, marching across this sunniest of days like
a resolute black rain-cloud. The moment of contentment
is mercilessly smothered. Where brightness and warmth
were just seconds ago, there is now only a depressing
chill.

Many who walk backwards feel that they can silence the whispering accusations in their minds by pushing themselves to new heights of holiness and piety. If they just pray more, witness more, give more, perhaps that taunting voice will be silenced. They redouble their efforts in relationships: perhaps if they can just keep up the act, they will be accepted. But no. Indeed, the victims of false guilt can fall prey to a circular, twisted logic which leads them, ironically, back into sin: 'I have sinned. Even though I have sought and begged and craved forgiveness, my past sin still mocks and torments me. So, even in my present state of pristine purity, I still feel smeared. What then is the point of purity? To hell with it.'

Then, to add insult to injury, the joyless guilty discover a new source of guilt – they don't live joyful Christian lives! We always hear that we are supposed to be full of peace, so our anxiety doubles as we identify, instead, our restlessness. If we experience a period of relief from our guilt, we even feel guilty about that! Unresolved guilt brings us to the place where we really can't win.

The destroyer of life

Some people lose joy – and some even lose their lives as a result of self-condemnation. James Dobson sums up the horror of it

> Self condemnation gnaws on the conscious mind by day and invades the dreams by night. For some particularly vulnerable individuals, an internal taskmaster is on the job from early morning until late at night – screaming accusations at his tormented victim.

John – not his real name – was a bright, popular guy who seemed to enjoy his work as an associate pastor in the church across town in the English Midlands. I never knew him that well, but he seemed to be intelligent and confident, enjoying life. But his smile masked an inner darkness. Prior to entering full-time Christian ministry, John had lived for a year or two in a state of open rebellion towards God. He wasn't just immoral – he was perversely immoral in his passion for sexual deviancy. Then John came back to God. His repentance was total, his commitment unquestioned. But the sickening images of his past stained his soul. Try as he might, he couldn't forget the evil in his personal history. He became convinced that he had blasphemed the Holy Spirit, that he had bypassed the possibility of forgiveness, even though his life and conduct clearly showed that the Holy Spirit was working overtime in his life and had been for years.

My telephone screamed at 3 am. It was John's minister. John had disappeared, leaving a note on his door: 'Burn my clothes, and consign my soul to hell.'

He read in his Bible that some would be saved, but only by fire. He put his Bible down. He wrote his note. He went out into a lonely, windswept field, poured a can of petrol over his head and burned himself to death. This was no quiet, calm martyr's death – he breathed his last in agony.

Perhaps John stepped over the threshold into mental illness: who knows what drives people when they find themselves in such deep personal despair? But, whatever the final diagnosis, one thing is sure: false guilt was his executioner.

False guilt. Not just something I should endure, perversely, for his Name's sake.

Not just an incidental problem for the spiritually sensitive.

False guilt. Brutal murderer. John's killer.

Chapter 3

True or false?

*Human beings are the only animals that blush
or need to.*

Mark Twain

Our culture has declared war on all forms of guilt. One best-selling author declares that guilt is 'the most useless of all erroneous zone behaviours. Guilt zones must be exterminated, spray cleaned and sterilised forever'.[6] But, according to the new gurus, this 'spray cleaning' will not happen as we honestly repent of our sins and seek forgiveness. Rather, our salvation comes, we are told, as we realise that *all* guilt is negative – an idea completely at odds with biblical Christianity. But the message is popular nonetheless. Even Ann Landers, once the advice column queen of America, says

> One of the most painful, self mutilating, time and energy consuming exercises in the human experience is guilt. It can ruin your day – or your week or your life – if you let it. It turns up like a bad penny when you do something dishonest, hurtful, tacky, selfish or rotten . . . never mind that it was the result of ignorance, thoughtlessness, weak

flesh, or clay feet. You did wrong and the guilt is killing you. Too bad. But be assured, the agony you feel is normal. Remember that guilt is a pollutant and we don't need any more of it in the world.[7]

The same message is being sold to the youth culture. MTV once aired a special programme entitled *The Seven Deadly Sins* but according to the MTV moguls, sin is anything but deadly. The programme attempted to sum up our post-modern attitude towards morality, and featured interviews with well-known celebrities as well as ordinary people out shopping. The whole thing was mixed as a collage, with video clips from well-known movies. Here is a sample of their 'words of wisdom'[8]

> *Pride is a sin? I wasn't aware of that . . .*
> Rap singer, Queen Latifah

> *I don't think pride is a sin, and I think some idiot made that up. Who made all these up?*
> Actress, Kirstie Alley

A perceptive review of the MTV programme appeared in US News and World Report, saying

> 'There's a vague sense that sin, if it exists, is surely a problem of psychology.' Kurt Loder, the narrator, says, '. . . The seven deadly sins are not evil acts, but, rather, universal human compulsions that can be troubling and highly enjoyable.'

The message is plain. All the bad feelings we have about ourselves are unhealthy. Get rid of these feelings – and get better. But the foolishness of this argument is immediately obvious. True guilt is actually a sign of nobility, a hint from heaven that we are more than mere animals. We weep as we think of naked Jewish women being herded to the gas chambers by Nazi guards who shed no tears of remorse for what they were doing. But we mourn for those guards as well as their helpless victims: their hard-hearted Nazi stoicism was testimony to their brutalised depravity, not some beautiful 'advanced' dignity.

The trend is to reject as valueless *all* guilt, both good and bad. Indeed, sometimes we punish the victim, and applaud and excuse the criminal. The 'All guilt is wrong, I'm a sinner and proud of it' message is pumped out daily. *Oprah* and a host of other programmes provide regular platforms for people to confess their lurid sins with pride – and, more often than not, to be applauded by an excited studio audience as they do so. Our tele-confessions make us the opposite of our Victorian ancestors who tried to exorcise their demons with manic cover-up, draping even the legs of wooden tables lest they offend the modest! Our culture is more like a street-wise whore than a blushing virgin. Daytime television allows us to throw open the darkest caverns of our souls to the watching, salivating millions. As we make our heart an open house, we receive a reward. To confess to adultery and perversion, greed and deception, is seen as 'courageous.'

'Confession' without the need for change is popular. 'Confession 900' telephone services are big business in the US – huge profits can be creamed from a bumper harvest of guilt. You can phone in and 'confess' to a gentle, computerised voice – or listen to the confessions of others – and all for two dollars for the first minute and forty-five cents per minute thereafter. A game for fools? An estimated 14,000 people call these lines every day.

But doesn't this render confession vain, an act of voyeurism as one person's sins are used to titillate and arouse a paying listener?

Guilt won't lie down and die, and God forbid the day that it does. As someone put it simply, 'It's good to feel guilty when you are.' Instead of declaring war on *all* forms of shame and guilt, we need to learn the difference between *good* and *bad* guilt – or between *conviction* and *condemnation*, if you prefer terms that Christians tend to use. If we don't discover this difference, we shall be forever confused.

Conviction comes from heaven; condemnation is spawned in hell – *but they both tend to provoke the same feelings*. And feelings are, according to William Gaylin, 'mushy, difficult, non-palpable, slippery . . . Difficult to quantify, difficult to communicate, difficult even to distinguish within ourselves one from the other.' Ultimately we need to understand that *feeling* bad doesn't necessarily mean that we are bad. In biblical terms, guilt is more about actions than feelings.

> It is significant to note that of the three New Testament words translated 'guilt' in our language (*hupodikos*, *opheilo* and *enochos*), not one refers to the feeling of guilt. Instead, they mean 'to be liable of judgement', 'to be guilty of an offence' or 'to owe or be indebted to'. When God speaks of guilt, he is refering to true, actual guilt, not an emotional state.[9]

> The distinction between the two [good and bad guilt] is commonly blurred in people's minds. It is important to know when guilt is a help and when it is a hindrance. For it can be both. We need to remember guilt's duality in order to engage it head on. Otherwise guilt is just an incomprehensible enemy, always lying in wait to attack.[10]

It isn't enough just to hear the message that provokes feelings of guilt: I need to ask where that message is coming from. If someone I respect and trust rebukes me for some slippage in my character, I am more inclined to take a positive view of their criticism and make a quick response. I know the messenger and what motivates them – love for me and a desire to help. But if I receive an anonymous letter full of irate, ungracious complaint (as I sometimes do!) from someone who is angry because my preaching seems to have made them uncomfortable, I am less willing to accept their judgement. The letter's author hasn't been courageous enough to make themselves known to me; I don't know their heart and their message seems more inspired by a Pharisaical attitude than genuine love for God, concern for me or a desire to be constructive.

Jiminy Cricket got it wrong

Pinocchio was obviously a great sinner – that's how he got a telescopic nose. But, thankfully, he was rescued from his deceptive ways by a little insect with a moral heart and a catchy tune: 'Always let your conscience be your guide!' Though some believers seem to think that this saying about the conscience is biblical, we should take care: God didn't say those words – Jiminy Cricket did. The great J.B. Phillips comments

> [To] make conscience into God is a highly dangerous thing to do. For one thing . . . conscience is by no means an infallible guide; and for another it is extremely unlikely that we shall ever be moved to worship, love, and serve a nagging inner voice that at worst spoils our pleasure and at best keeps us rather negatively on the

path of virtue. Conscience can be so easily perverted or morbidly developed in the sensitive person, and so easily ignored and silenced by the insensitive, that it makes a very unsatisfactory god. For while it is probably true that every normal person has an embryo moral sense by which he can distinguish right and wrong, the development, non development, or perversion of that sense is largely a question of upbringing, training and propaganda.[11]

The Bible places enormous value on us having a clear conscience, but never suggests that our conscience is a foolproof, infallible guide. There are people who have a 'seared conscience'. They sin with enthusiasm and almost no regret. Consider the chilling psychopathic killer, Dr Hannibal Lecter, in the film *The Silence of the Lambs*. His despicable crimes cause him no qualms of guilt: he licks his lips and remembers the pain he has inflicted with a sense of luxury rather than with any hint of anguish or regret. He is suffering from *superego lacunae* – holes in the conscience. And, sadly, we all know that there really are Lecters out there – Fred and Rosemary West, Ian Brady, Myra Hindley, Harold Shipman . . . Always let your conscience be your guide?

> In Nazi Germany, propaganda as a weapon to pervert the moral sense became a fine art. It soon seemed, for example, a positive duty to hate the Jews, and a good Nazi would doubtless have suffered pangs of conscience if he had been kind to one of the despised race.[12]

To go to the other extreme, Scripture teaches that there are those who have a 'weak conscience', who rush to repent of anything, including a lot of things that aren't sinful. A friend of ours was once nearly knocked down by a speeding motorist, who screamed abuse out of his window as he drove on. Even though she was entirely in the right, his words dug deep into her and brought to the surface illogical feelings of shame.

Pauline, a Jehovah's Witness, knocked on our door to sell us a copy of *The Watchtower* magazine. Exhausted by nineteen tedious years of loveless religion, she began a friendship with Jesus Christ. She quickly led other members of her immediate family to faith, and it wasn't long before we had a row of ex-Jehovah's Witnesses in our church. All of them were 'disfellowshipped' – excommunicated from the Kingdom Hall.

Pauline and the group grew quickly in their new faith: they relished their freedom and were eager to learn. Everything went well until Christmas. Pauline was excited about celebrating her first Christmas in nearly two decades. The green spruce Christmas tree stood proud and tall in her home, a symbol of her newfound liberty. And then, the day before Christmas Eve, her husband phoned me, his voice signalling alarm. Pauline was running around the house, frantically collecting up all their Christmas cards and throwing them out of the window. And it looked like the brightly decorated tree was going to be next, lights and glitter and all. What was wrong? For years her tender conscience had been programmed, drip-fed the belief that Christmas was evil and now she was having a panic attack over what is an essentially neutral issue. The voice of religious training had come to sound like the voice of God.

Even those who seem strong can be smitten by a weak conscience. William Cowper was one of the greatest poets and hymn-writers of the eighteenth century. Majestic songs celebrating God's mercy and forgiveness flowed from his pen

There is a fountain filled with Blood
Drawn from Emmanuel's veins
And sinners plunged beneath that flood
Lose all their guilty stains.

E'er since by faith I saw the stream
Thy flowing wounds supply
Redeeming love has been my theme
And shall be till I die.

But Cowper, cursed with a weak conscience, never felt he had lost all his 'guilty stains'. Wracked by terrible periods of depression that drove him to attempt suicide, he was convinced he could never be forgiven for his iniquities and called himself 'damned beyond Judas'. Even Cowper's close friend John Newton, writer of 'Amazing Grace', was unable to assure him that he was saved. He didn't die with love as his recurring theme: he died believing that he was beyond forgiveness. As James Dobson says, 'The conscience is an imperfect mental faculty. There are times when it condemns us for mistakes and human frailties that can't be avoided; at other times it will remain silent in the face of indescribable wickedness.'[13]

This is one of the reasons why discipleship is so important. Dumping a Bible and a church service schedule into a new believer's hands and leaving them to fend for themselves is nothing short of criminal. Condemnation can cripple someone with a weak conscience, particularly when they isolate the signals their conscience is sending them and don't take other factors into consideration. An educated and informed conscience, nourished by truth, balanced by friendship, responsive to conviction, aware of the fraudulent claims of condemnation: this is a good conscience.

A sign that something specific is wrong

I spend a great deal of time behind the steering wheel of my car, travelling to and from meetings. Because I spend many hours on the road, I know pretty well what my car feels and sounds like when I drive it. Once when I was motoring along I became aware that something was wrong, but I didn't know what. The steering wheel shook slightly; the noise of the tyres on the road surface was a little different in tone. Something was definitely amiss.

Choosing to ignore it, I drove the three hundred miles home. When I got out of the car I discovered, to my horror, that my back tyre was so bald the canvas inner lining was sticking out. I had driven down the motorway at high speed. Ignoring the warning signs could have cost me dearly.

It is the 'gift' of pain that insists you take your hand off a hot stove. To be without it is to be like the leper who is unable to feel anything in their extremities. Because of this, there is no danger signal to warn them when they injure themselves, and they lose fingers and toes as a result. Pain can work for our benefit – it is an announcement that something is wrong and needs to be put right. Guilt can serve the same purpose, guiding us away from sin, preserving wholeness and integrity, driving us back to God and to goodness again.

To go back to my experience with the car, the warning signs told me to change the tyre, not scrap the car! True conviction or positive guilt is like that: God allows us to feel challenged about specific areas of our behaviour, offering a focused sense of shame about our sins and prompting us towards a positive outcome. However, false guilt has a generally smothering effect: rather than pinpointing a specific issue, it throws a blanket of condemnation over us and suffocates us with universal shame and a feeling of hopelessness. Positive guilt says, 'This action/habit is wrong and needs to be put right.' False guilt says, 'You as a person are all wrong, bad, useless and will probably never be right, no matter how hard you strive.'

A step up, not a step back

Condemnation, far from enhancing our sense of dignity and worth, shouts that our sin is really no surprise because trash produces trash. We are led away from salvation and left angry, despairing and empty.

Condemnation demands that we 'clean up' before we go anywhere near the Father. We try to live for God in order to make him love us, hoping that our pristine performance will one day make him accept us. Sadly, for the soul tormented by condemnation, that bright day never seems to dawn.

Ironically, condemnation may actually lead us into gross immorality. Exhausted by continuous emotional whippings and crippled by our sense of unworthiness, we give up and desperately try to fill the sadness in our hearts with food, sex, chemicals, money, abusive and self-destructive habits, so hungry are we for relief from our feelings of guilt. And why not? If I really am just a worthless worm, I might as well do what worms are good at – squirm around in the dirt. If God has a permanent frown and nothing about me will ever bring a smile to his face, why pretend to purity? If I feel vaguely mediocre all the time, if I despair of my own ability to improve myself and doubt God's willingness to help me, why struggle and strain towards excellence? This is why we shouldn't be surprised when incest and abuse emerge in intensely legalistic churches, or when 'holiness' evangelists are caught consorting with prostitutes. Grace has been sent packing by the spirit of false religion, and people have had the hope hammered out of them. There is nothing left to feel but despair: false guilt, disguised as the Spirit of God, has done its work.

Condemnation is the stone in your shoe that just won't go away. It cuts into you at every step, every time you remember the failures of your past. It is a foolproof strategy for torment and punishment, since time-travel is still beyond us: no one can really go back to the past and put their mistakes right. God never invites us to walk backwards into guilt. If we repented back then, we were forgiven back then. God doesn't just forget our sins, like an absent-minded judge: rather, he chooses to deliberately remember our sins *no more*. And it is impossible for him to go into the business of reminding us about them – to do so would be a violation of all that he is and all that he says of himself in Scripture. Condemnation is upside-down Christianity, good news turned very bad.

Conviction, on the other hand, comes with the opportunity to be enfolded by the warm, forgiving arms of a loving God. The Holy Spirit shows us our sins, not because we are worthless but because God sees us, by his grace, as being so worthwhile. We are shown that our sinful behaviour is incompatible with our position as God's children. Under conviction, we see that we have stooped down to sin; but we receive an instant invitation to *step up* out of the mire and the muck of sin's pigpen and back into the warmth of the Father's house.

Conviction is the sharp scalpel of healing that cuts us when we sin. Conviction comes not to punish us by making us feel bad – rather, the uncomfortable feelings we experience are redemptive, designed to prod us into repentance and thereafter grace.

Conviction is God calling us to take a specific, reachable step with him, like a child crossing a river hand in hand with his father. Confident of Dad's loving grasp, the child's feet skip over the slippery stepping-stones. Thus God takes us by the hand and helps us over the river of guilt towards mercy and forgiveness. Through conviction, he calls us to freedom.

Conviction comes with the knowledge that God loves us utterly and completely as we are. He will never love you any more than he does right at this moment. But God loves us too much to let us remain trapped in our wrong behaviour. Conviction is God's kiss, not his punch, a hug for the filthy prodigal before he has a bath. We live for God *because* we are loved, not in order to be loved (1 John 4:19).

Conviction brings us face to face with Christ. Condemnation is essentially Christ-less, driving us away from him into the sewer of our own attempts at self-sufficiency. Estranged from the warmth of the Lord Jesus, we march sternly and resolutely towards a sterile personal morality, our chests swelling with pride at every achievement. But conviction drives us not just to principle and precept and law, but to the strong person of Christ himself. Humble and broken, but with his hand in ours, we are restored.

An offer, not a bill

The words 'guilt' and 'gold' both come from the same Anglo-Saxon word, *gylt*, meaning 'to pay'. Condemnation presents us with a six-figure invoice which is overwhelming: if we work twenty-fours hours a day for ever, we will never, never clear the debt – the interest due is more than our monthly repayment. Condemnation has done its wicked work well – the need to pay is endemic to our humanity.

The need to pay. See it in the eyes of the person who receives a surprise gift – it isn't their birthday or Christmas. See the discomfort, the embarrassment: 'Oh, you shouldn't have. I didn't get you anything.' As they grow into adulthood, people often leave behind the child's ability to receive freely, and develop a sophisticated uneasiness towards simple acts of kindness and grace. Soon we become cynical, adopting as our slogan 'Nothing in life is free.' Our hearts are hardened by the slick soliciting of advertisers who send us 'free' gifts with a catch, until we reach the inevitable, sad conclusion that free gifts don't exist. No wonder we struggle with the God who offers forgiveness for free!

The need to pay. See it in the eyes of the religious penitent. Some friends of mine went on a medical mission to the garbage dumps of Mexico City. They wept as they ministered to people who lived their whole lives in makeshift homes of rubbish, scooping trash with their bare hands for thirty pence a day. But it wasn't only the garbage township that caused my friends distress: the basilica in the centre of city, far from being a citadel of hope in a dark place, cast its own oppressive shadow. My friends watched helplessly as the pious faithful crawled painfully on their knees across the rough cobblestones into the imposing building, some with babies in their arms. Their crawl was a desperate sob for mercy in the forlorn hope that if they made this bruising payment to heaven, mercy would be forthcoming.

The need to pay. See it in the eyes of the critical, self-assured Christian in some American 'holiness' church, who prides herself that she doesn't attend movies, wear make-up, watch television, go bowling, wear jewellery, or indeed do anything that could be remotely identified as fun. See it in the young man appalled and outraged by the music at a Christian festival: it was too loud, the words were unclear, the sound too contemporary and, dear God, people were dancing – and *not in worship!* The possibility that it might be appropriate for Christians just to enjoy themselves without some blatantly obvious religious reason for doing so was beyond him. In his sincerity he put joy, spontaneity and laughter on hold, postponing them until after death, reserving them for another world.

Conviction brings us to the wonderful realisation that we are blessedly helpless and impotent. As we ponder the overwhelming bill, we realise our total inability to settle the account. To even begin writing the cheque would reveal a preposterous pride in our hearts.

> On the day I was born, God danced.
> Did you really, God? Was it a ritualistic,
>   dignified, bow-from-the-waist kind of dance?
> Or was it just possibly a wild and crazy
> arm flinging kind of thing?
> Did you pronounce sombrely
> that here was another 'good girl'
> that you had created?
> Or did you yell and holler and
> grab the guy on the corner
> to let him know this time
> you had really done it!
> This time you created a winner –
> This one was going to go all the way!
> I hope you did, God –
> I really hope you did.

Sarah Hall Maney[14]

34

Chapter 4

The enemy

Satan is a liar. One day he will be thrown into a lake of fire. Next time Satan tries to remind you about your past, go ahead and remind him about his future.

Jack Hayford

Satan. Cue spooky music and distant screams in the inky black night. Billows of silver-lined fog swirl around the deserted graveyard. Crucifix in hand, the caped and hooded priest hurries through the crooked tombstones to exorcise a demented toddler's demons. Religious fervour dances in his wide-eyed stare. He loves his work . . .

Satan. A long thin leer of a face. Cat's eyes, sulphur yellow and black. Thin lips, framed by a goatee beard, stretched tight in a smile with the hint of a sneer. Foetid, sulphurous breath. Horned head, hoofed feet. Stated fashion preference – a red cape. Standard equipment – three pronged pitchfork, handy for poking the damned and stoking the coals.

Satan. We're tempted to leave him in a Hollywood studio back-lot, to be stacked alongside Superman, Mickey

Mouse and Santa Claus. Even our post-modern culture, with its enthusiasm for almost any belief system, struggles with the Christian theology of Satan – although Satanism itself seems to be acceptable. A Christian who admits in public that they actually believe in the existence of a specific personality known as 'the devil' may be suspected of also harbouring a belief in the tooth fairy. Images of devils and demons are just too medieval and primitive to be treated seriously. Believe in 'old Nick'? What a quaint, superstitious and possibly dangerous notion. Let me help you put your straitjacket on . . .

Even some clergy have 'outgrown' the devil. 'Satan' is just a word, they protest with a cough of embarrassment – a metaphor, a figure of speech for evil. So we are left with a Jesus who spent a third of his ministry misguidedly doing battle with someone who wasn't real, a Christ who cast a metaphor into a herd of pigs which ran headlong down a hillside and drowned. Time-wasting, dangerous things, these metaphors.

As blind sophistication clouds our eyes to the devil, Satan laughs triumphantly. He would have us either obsessed with him or oblivious to his presence: either way he is able to work unhindered. People may snigger and accuse us of believing in a cartoon character, but the truth is this – Satan is all too real. His foul handiwork is evident everywhere. He scrawls his signature on the hollow faces of the hungry who die in the shadows of Western food mountains, pyramids in honour of greed. He rests a hand of gentle approval on the shoulder of the pornographer who films the violating and slaying of children, lambs ushered without mercy to the slaughterhouse. He smiles serenely as the teenager sears his nostrils and then his brain with cocaine. The silent screams of the aborted millions fill his ears as a sweet serenade.

Christians affirm that there is evil in the world and this evil is more than just an impersonal force operating in the hearts of humankind. We know that there is a general of arms, a warrior of wickedness, who carries the name 'Satan.' A belief in a personal God is only part of the Christian gospel. 'A belief in a personal devil and demon activities is the touchstone by which we can most easily test any profession of Christian faith today' said Martyn Lloyd-Jones.

The struggles and pressures of the Christian life only make sense when we understand that Satan exists as our sworn enemy. Christianity isn't 'nice', despite the prevailing images that cling to faith: cosy afternoon tea with the kindly but irrelevant vicar, blue-rinse grannies knitting doilies for the missionaries, Sunday School kids singing 'All things bright and beautiful' endearingly out of tune. These warm, safe pictures belie the truth: to be a Christian is to live in a state of open warfare. Unfortunately, 'much of the church's warfare today is fought by blindfolded soldiers who cannot see the forces ranged against them, who are buffeted by invisible opponents and respond by striking one another' according to Richard Lovelace.

But let's not make the devil too large or pay him overmuch attention, as some have done. Christians preoccupied with a super-sized Satan turn their lives into one long demon safari. Take the rather overweight worship leader whose belt snapped as he led singing for a Sunday morning meeting. His voluminous trousers slid in a moment down his legs, revealing some rather spectacular boxer shorts apparently designed by Walt Disney. The leaders who were unfortunate enough to be sitting on the platform immediately stuffed handkerchiefs, fists, even Bibles into their mouths to gag raucous and shoulder-shaking laughter. Undeterred, the hapless and trouserless brother leaned into the microphone and declared gravely, 'It's amazing what the devil will do to you when you're trying to worship . . .' The possibility that his bulging waistline may have contributed something to the strain on his overworked belt never entered his thinking. That nasty devil had broken through again. God help the trousers of the man who isn't sufficiently spiritual.

The battle is no equal contest. Satan is a pygmy compared to the muscle and mind of our God, so don't give the devil credit where credit isn't due. God alone is omnipotent (all powerful): Satan has to run for his life when even we resist him (Jas. 4:7). God alone is omnipresent (everywhere at all times): Satan may be looking for someone to devour, but note that he has to 'prowl around' in order to do this (1 Pet. 5:8) – he is limited to one location at a time. God alone is transcendent (high and lifted up): Satan fell out of heaven like lightning that screams and sears its way from the clouds to the earth in a second (Luke 10:18). Most of us have never met and will never meet him in person: we don't merit his personal attention that much. Rather, our skirmishes tend to be with the demonic soldiers that march in his name.

Though Satan does need to be cut down to size, the fact remains that he does exist and he has a very detailed, specific agenda. It is when we understand who and what our enemy is that we learn not to be surprised by his tactics. To get a handle on his strategy, climb inside the Beelzebub brain for a moment.

I had everything. I was the most favoured cherub, conductor of the symphonies of millions as they romanced him with music that shook mountains. I was his confidante and chief courtier in his throne room; his ear was mine. I spent glorious ages basking in luxurious, extravagant joy. I enjoyed a privileged existence, privy to the archangels' whispers, present as the prayers of the faithful drifted up like incense.

I had everything. My dazzling beauty was so majestic, super-beings gasped at my brilliant splendour. My name was a song on their lips. Angel of Light, they called me, Lucifer.

I had everything, but it was not enough. I dreamed of the day when his throne could be mine. I imagined those same songs of worship, but with *me* as their object of adoration. I will climb onto the highest clouds, I said to myself. 'Let angels and men celebrate *my* name! Let them cry, "Here comes the Judge" when *I* walk by!'

These thoughts lingered and became a dark obsession. I set out to pursue the dream that pride had planted. Gathering followers for my coup was easy: I was so impressive, so persuasive. Yet even as I embroidered my clever speeches and staked my claim, I knew that it was hopeless. Who can stand against him?

His judgement fell upon my neck like an axe, razor sharp and swift.

Now I am exiled from love, a prodigal angel, fallen and homeless. The Angel of Light is no more: now

I am Beelzebub, Lord of the Dunghill. Once toasted by winged warriors, I am now Lord of the Flies. The spoils of my vain rebellion? The rotten, putrid, decaying kingdom of darkness. I am the first-fruit of all in human history who took the love of the Most High and spat on it. At the end of all things, we who have rebelled will be together, the congregation of fugitives from heaven.

So I, heaven's castaway, will bar the entrance to those heavenly courts. I will do everything in my power to slam shut those golden gates. I will take the holiness of God that banished me and twist it to deceive the faithful. Against the foolish I will wield the blunt weapon of temptation – lurid pornographic incitements to draw them into my twilight zone. I will need no finesse or sophistication to woo them. How easily, how predictably they stumble into sin. I will peddle the doctrines of demons to entice those searching for him. I will seize those seeking his presence and fill their hearts with pride. I will invite them to strut before him, 'justified' by their capacity to stick to endless rules and regulations. Their own piety will blind them to the face of Christ.

How will I obstruct those won over by his love, those tender-hearted souls too holy for much sin, too humble for much pride? For them I reserve my most brilliant strategy: I will *shame* them. I can never be their judge, so I will appoint myself their prosecutor. And because of this I will be called Satan. Slanderer. Accuser. I will torment them with the fiery darts of the knowledge of their imperfection. I will overwhelm them with the facts of their own histories. I will present concrete evidence of their sins, but with one thing missing. Grace. The grace that can never be mine.

I will use my mastery of impersonation to make it seem as though it is *their God* who accuses them. I will sow the seeds of hatred in their hearts. Some will shrink from him in fear and remain strangers to Christ's promise. Others will grow weary of their faith.

I will terrorise and dominate his children – and I will do it with a whisper . . .

Whispers in your mind

Smith Wigglesworth was one of God's wild men. Bold and eccentric, astonishing miracles punctuated his ministry. But those who would taste victory must make their home on the battlefield; Wigglesworth soon became a satanic target. The story is told of how this uneducated plumber-apostle woke with a start in the middle of the night, disturbed by a noise at his bedside. Reaching for the lamp and rubbing the sleep from his eyes, he quickly saw the source of the sound. Satan – or an apparition of Satan – was standing at the foot of the bed.

Freeze the frame for a moment and put yourself in Wigglesworth's nightshirt. What would you do? Throw your Bible at the devil? Dive under the sheets? Scream for your mum? Do all three at once? Wigglesworth chose none of these options. He looked the sworn enemy of all things good in the eye and said, 'Oh, it's only you.' He then switched off the lamp, snuggled back down in the warmth of the blankets and went back to sleep . . .

It's a great and true story of a genuine hero of faith, but the reality of daily life is that Satan doesn't usually announce his presence with trumpet fanfares and vivid night-time apparitions. Such a strategy would be far too obvious. Rather, the devil is the master of disguise, subtlety and camouflage (2 Cor. 11:14), the proverbial salesman who could sell truckloads of sand to the Arabs. Satan knows that some fancy footwork is required if he is to hoodwink us and thus succeed in his task as our prosecuting attorney. So his method is quietly to build a sandcastle, a house of thoughts, in our minds. With great patience and cunning, with a whisper here, a hint there, Satan establishes frontiers in our thinking. Day after day, he digs trenches and strings barbed wire entanglements in the uncharted inner space deep inside our heads. Quietly he weaves webs of questions, doubts, fears, suggestions, arguments, insinuations. He fires no loud shots – that would alert us and put us on guard. Steadily he works towards his prize, and, at last, the sandcastle becomes a stronghold.

> The weapons we fight with are not the weapons of the world. On the contrary, they have divine power to demolish strongholds. We demolish arguments and every pretension that sets itself up against the knowledge of God, and we take captive every thought to make it obedient to Christ. (2 Cor. 10:4–5)

And what is Satan's favoured weapon as he lays claim to our thought-life? It is accusation, false guilt. Satan uses accusation so much he is even named in honour of the tactic: the word 'Satan' means 'Accuser.' So the Old Testament writers occasionally refer to their human enemies and accusers as 'satans' – five times the psalmist speaks of the human 'satans' who oppose him (Ps. 38:20;

71:13; 109:4,20,29). In his classic, *The Screwtape Letters*, C.S. Lewis describes the daily duties of a hardworking demon commissioned to trip up a faithful Christian by encouraging him to dwell constantly on his failures and inadequacies so that his whole existence is lived in guilt. The devil is sly, deceitful, wicked and clever – he has earned his satanic name. Just as the most prominent feature in God's character is his love, so the major chord in the discordant symphony that makes up Satan's personality is accusation.

God on trial

Ever since his meteoric fall, Satan has 'sataned.' Even the brightness of Eden's garden was dimmed by his shadow. Ironically, the first one in the dock was God himself (Gen. 3:1–5). In the courtroom he had skilfully erected in Eve's mind, the accuser slandered the Creator with outrageous audacity, overwhelming Eve with his blindingly subtle arguments.

There were two charges read out that day. Firstly, God was charged with being unreliable: 'Did God really say . . .?' (Are you sure that what God says is true anyway? Can his words be trusted? Did he really say what you think he said?) Secondly, God was accused of having smeared and selfish motives: 'If you eat the fruit, your eyes will be opened . . . God knows that you will be like him.' (God is more interested in his own self preservation than your welfare.)

The deception was remarkably effective – remember, Eve had taken late afternoon garden walks with God; she was close friends with him (Gen. 3:8). But still she was convinced by the cunning, smooth-talking prosecutor who is the father of lies (John 8:44). The one-woman jury reached her verdict. She ate, and then so did Adam. Eyes opened, case closed, Paradise lost.

Satan would like to recreate that courtroom triumph in *our* minds. He will tell us God's word can't be trusted; God can't be that wonderful; surely the idea of forgiveness is scandalous.[15] The serpent's hisses echo still: 'So, he said that you could be cleansed and forgiven, did he? How can that be true when you still feel so guilty? Surely the darkness of condemnation you feel right now is proof enough that his word isn't true?' Though Scripture shouts about God's amazing grace, endless mists of doubt swirl around our subconscious. Like Eve, if we lose sight of God's goodness, we will quickly lose the motivation to obey him.

Satan is history's most prolific and gifted prosecutor. He has handled cases against Job, Joshua, David. In the wilderness he came against Jesus (Matt. 4:1–11; Mark 1:9–13; Luke 4:1–13). Through the wagging tongues of the Pharisees, he accused and blasphemed the Holy Spirit (eg Luke 11:14–20). If the satanic attorney will point the finger at everyone – even the great Judge himself – isn't it more than likely that he will try to pull the same stunt on us?

The death of hope

Satan's strategy is wickedly clever because it destroys faith for the present and hope for the future. Suffocated by guilt, we feel powerless to effect any meaningful change in our world. If God hasn't forgiven me, then what is the point of anything?

Satan didn't even shrink from attempting to snatch hope from Jesus' heart. The Lord began his messianic ministry by asking his friend and cousin John to baptise him. Moments later, he emerged from the water soaked through and supernaturally assured. 'This is my beloved Son – I'm really pleased with him!' cried the Father. Affirmation. Hope. Salvation on the way.

'Prove it with some tricks. You're nobody. Worship me. Live for the now. You're hungry. Come on, be the miracle baker of Galilee.'

Like a character in a children's pop-up book, Satan appeared and bombarded Jesus with demonic questions about his identity, his mission, his strategy.

Thankfully, Jesus was confident enough in God to send the prosecutor packing with some well-chosen words. Hope still burned bright in his heart, and he was able to march on into his great mission.

Run away, Simba

The Lion King is one of my favourite movies – I can't watch it without shedding a few tears. Simba is a young lion cub, the son of the powerful king of the Pride Lands. In the film, his father is killed trying to save Simba during a stampede of buffalo. Perhaps one of the most poignant moments is when Simba, overwhelmed by grief over his father's death, is confronted by his uncle Scar, a dark satanic figure. Scar drapes Simba in shame, accusing him of being responsible for his father's death. In desperation, Simba cries out, 'What shall I do?' The reply was swift, the advice demonic: 'Run away, Simba, and never come back.' Tragically, the young lion who was born to be king wanders off into the loneliness of exile, banished from his rightful inheritance by guilt.

Fortunately, there is a happy ending. Years later, Simba meets a childhood friend who tries to persuade him to return and save the Pride Lands from the awful destruction of Scar's rule. However, he takes a lot of persuading. Simba still blames himself for his father's death and consequently has a very low opinion of himself – he feels weak and scared, even though he's now a full-grown lion and looks strong and brave. The decision hinges on an encounter he has with a wise monkey who knew Simba's father. Simba, who thinks the monkey is crazy, asks him, 'Who are you?'

The monkey replies, 'The question is, who are you?'

The monkey tells Simba that if he looks closely enough, he will see his father living in him. He takes the young lion to a pool and shows him his reflection. As Simba peers at it, he begins to see his resemblance to his father. He hears his father's voice saying, 'You are more than what you have become. Remember who you are. You are my son . . .' With this knowledge Simba's courage returns and he is able to go back to the Pride Lands, overthrow Scar and claim his rightful inheritance.

Imagine Adam and Eve diving for cover in Eden as they hear the sound of God's footsteps. See the tragic triumph of accusation's work. Convinced by Satan that God's heart was less than good, they crash through the undergrowth, desperate to cover their nakedness and shame, to flee from the presence of the Holy One. The accuser makes the drawing close to God that we call prayer a nightmare. Scripture becomes a legal document that sentences us every time we read it. Church meetings become a weekly session of agony. Eventually we are tempted to do what the voice says, to just run away and never come back.

But we need to remember who we are . . .

An endless, droning voice

We all remember the tedium of the infamous O.J. Simpson trial: for over a year lawyers sweated under the television lights, picking over the minutiae of the case. Similarly, Satan picks over the little details of our lives. He is repetitive in his strategy and persistent with his words, perfectly happy to rehearse the same old arguments and summations a million times. Satan is long-winded: Scripture tags him as the one who accuses us 'day and night.'

> Satan keeps a watchful eye on the soul, determining if it is blunted or sensitive. If sensitive, he works to the point of making it excessively refined so that he can more easily trouble or upset it. He will make the soul . . . imagine sins where there are none present . . .[16]

One writer describes Satan as 'the opposition party in God's parliament' – the endless, droning voice of the politician who mocks everything that comes from the other side of house. Some Christians teach that a thought which won't go away is probably from God. We need to be aware, however, that Satan is happy to go on and on harassing and debating. And the tragedy is that the real authority – the Judge – has already delivered his verdict. He has even written it in his book: case dismissed.

Chapter 5

People of grace or mercy-killers?

With a church like this, who needs Satan?
Clive Calver

My heart was beating wildly against my chest as I stepped into the crude, tin-roofed building. Out there in the foyer, I could hear their bright singing and hand clapping – a very strange sound. My only exposure to Christian services had been channel-surfing glimpses of *Songs of Praise*. Twenty years ago, it seemed that the BBC scoured the country every week and televised the most boring churches known to humanity. Even when the songs were up-tempo and the odd tambourine was flourished, the facial expressions of the camera-conscious congregation suggested that they had collectively had their feet run over by a large truck. I had not been impressed. Now, as I stood in this real live church building, aware that an 'usher' was bearing down on me with a warm smile and matching handshake, I knew this was not going to be *Songs of Praise*.

With an encouraging nod the usher held back a red velvet curtain, and I stepped through it into an alien world. A man at the front with wild, windmill arms was leading the singing and wrestling with a smile that threatened to take over his whole face. The organ soared. Many of the congregation, eyes moist and bright, had their arms raised in the air.

Hands up? Who were they waving at? Was this the religious method of asking permission to slip out to the loo: one hand if you needed to go a little, two hands if you needed to go *right now*?

Eyes shut tight now, some murmured quiet 'Amens', while – most bizarre – some appeared to know how to mutter in Russian, or was it German? Cantonese? By now I was succumbing to confusion, but it was to get worse. Abruptly the song ended, everyone sat down, and it was then that I saw it. What on earth were this lot playing at? Who in their right mind would build a miniature *swimming pool* in their church building? Walking-on-water lessons perhaps?

The minister appeared, dressed in a long black gown with fishing-waders up to his thighs. He looked like an aquatic Dracula. Stepping into the pool, he adjusted his gown and stood there, waiting. Another man joined him in the water, only he wore white. An air of expectancy crackled among the crowd – something important was going to happen. Suddenly Rev Dracula grabbed the hapless guy and pushed him under the water. His victim smiled just before he went under, smiled while underwater, and coughed, spluttered and smiled as he came back up, gasping. He had been baptised, and I had had enough. I fidgeted my way though the sermon, made a mental note of how many people were desperate to be excused during the final song, and left the place quickly, vowing never to return. Sitting outside in my car, I made what I thought was a life choice. Christians were crazy. I would have nothing to do with them ever again. I would drive off into the night and abandon the idea of faith.

Then I realised I'd left my coat in the church building.

I crept back inside and was immediately assaulted by the youth leader. Impossibly, he had a grin that outshone all the others. I had never seen so many teeth in a human head in my whole life. He asked if I would like to go to the 'afterglow.' I had no idea what he was on about, and secretly feared that this crowd ended their day by setting fire to old ladies. But I felt too intimidated to protest. Atheistic vows shattered by his kind persuasion, I walked in and joined the 'afterglowers.'

It was then that Dracula's victim approached me. Still wet, he shook my hand and got straight to the point: 'Pleased to meet you, Jeff. Are you are a Christian?' I searched frantically for a reply and mumbled something pathetic – of course I was a Christian, thank you, because isn't everyone who's British a Christian really – and realised that I wasn't a Christian and that, for some deep reason I couldn't explain, I wanted to know God. These people confused and irritated me, but I had to find out the reason for their smiles, which I knew were for real. I told my still-dripping friend that despite my British pedigree, I *wasn't* a Christian. I knew I wanted God, and asked him how to make the big step. His delighted smile warmed me, his words chilled me: 'You have to go to the little room at the back . . .'

Horrors. It was probably where they kept Dracula. It would be filled with stainless steel cabinets, glinting surgical knives and other instruments of torture. But I still wanted to become a Christian, so . . .

In that 'little room' my damp friend explained the gospel in a way that seemed to make complete sense, without the aid of syringes or rubber gloves. He told me about the wonderful Jesus who was waiting to step into my life, but only at my request. I hurried to my knees to issue the invitation.

It was now 10 pm. I was a Christian. Thrusting a Bible into one hand and grasping the other in a handshake of congratulation, my now dry counsellor opened the vestry door and I stepped out into what I thought would be an empty church building.

Then I saw them all and heard the cheer.

Every single one of those people had waited to welcome me into the family of God. With undisguised delight they had formed a long queue that stretched all the way to the back of the building. As I slowly went down that line of love, I was hugged, affirmed, received as a new brother. I had found a good church family, a real live community of grace.

But the sad reality is that not all have shared my experience.

> You don't have to be Jewish to be an expert in guilt. Catholics often outdo Jews in their ability to create guilt and, long after Martin Luther and Jonathan Edwards, Protestants still know guilt. And Moslems too. What do these religions have in common? Guilt. We are all experts in guilt.[17]

Church for some has been a place where they have learned how to feel bad on a consistent basis. Some churches seem to delight in reminding sinners of their sin. Though they speak of the doctrine of grace, for them grace is such an abstract, faraway idea that, week in, week out, the guilty are condemned with sickening regularity. It is a hideous tragedy to consider how many of those who profess to be followers of Christ live their whole lives in the shadowy catacombs of religious condemnation. The Church becomes an army of penniless millionaires – rich in grace, yet squandering their wealth because of the sense of shame that covers them.

51

I hate to put it so bluntly, but some churches lead people to a diminished conversion experience, and these converts to shame feel diminished for the rest of their lives as a result. One new Christian put it like this: 'Before I was a Christian I didn't feel so bad. Now I feel like the ball in a pinball machine, getting hit and bounced around from one guilt trip to another. The more I learn about believing in God, the more I feel guilty. The more I read my Bible or go to church, the more I feel guilty. I feel guilty about a lot of things a lot of the time.'[18] Another said sadly, 'Every time we go to church, the pastor spanks us.'[19]

Religion can be a sophisticated, well-oiled guilt machine. I have heard preachers who have sharply honed their shaming skills, who have the dubious gift of being able to smother vast crowds in guilt with their damning oratory.

> Ministers often use false guilt in attempting to control their congregations. They intercede in place of God, asking or demanding that they, not God, be the authority in people's lives. These ministers act out of fear, insecurity, and the need for power – not love. They attempt to manipulate God's love as they hide from their own feelings. As a result, they cripple people, keeping them from developing a true understanding of God and a healthy relationship with him.[20]

Obsessed with conformity

The pastor was horrified. 'Who is this?' he demanded, ignoring Roger completely. I started to introduce my friend, but before I could get any further, the irritated pastor spat out another question: 'Is he going to preach?'

Minutes earlier Roger and I had walked into his office to begin a four-day series of special evangelistic meetings. I hadn't reckoned on the negative reaction my friend was provoking. Why the unwelcoming outburst? Roger is a widely respected leader: what was the reason for this hostile reception?

Well, actually Roger was guilty of one significant crime. He was wearing his hair in a pony-tail.

He wasn't wearing the uniform of conservative evangelicalism, so he projected a somewhat 'radical' image at odds with what this particular minister thought appropriate for someone preaching God's word.

I have been deeply disturbed, particularly during my travels in the USA, by the clone-making tendencies of some fundamentalist churches. It worries me when I see young teenage guys uncomfortably togged up in awkward suits on Sunday mornings, as if they must participate in the culture of another generation in order to 'follow Jesus.' If they don't, they are accused of being 'rebellious.' Rebellious against whom, I ask?

The spirit of conservatism seems to endorse this smothering commitment to sameness, bringing a pressure to look like, sound like, act like and be like those around us. I was criticised in one church for using the word 'radical' in connection with Jesus. I was advised that this word had unfortunate political connotations. But Jesus was and is the most radical person there has ever been! He refused to bow down to legalistic posturing or to play religious mind-games. They wouldn't have crucified him otherwise.

Chuck Swindoll recognised and exposed this graceless conformity

For some reason . . . we are uneasy with differences. We prefer sameness, predictability, common

53

interests. If someone thinks differently or makes different choices than we do, prefers different entertainment, wears different clothing, has different tastes and opinions, or enjoys a different style of life, most Christians get nervous. We place far too much weight on externals and the importance of appearances, and not nearly enough on individuality and variety. We have acceptable norms in which we are able to move freely and allow others the freedom to do so. But heaven help the poor soul who steps beyond these bounds!

We compare musical tastes. We compare financial incomes. We compare marital status. We compare spirituality on the basis of externals. If an individual appreciates hymns and mellow songs, fine. If another prefers jazz or rock, watch out. The worst part of all of this is that it nullifies grace. It was never God's intention for all His children to look alike or embrace identical lifestyles. Look at the natural world He created. What variety! The buzzard and the butterfly . . . the dog and the deer . . . the zinnia and the orchid . . . the wriggling minnow and the sleek shark.

The church is not a religious industry designed to turn out mass produced reproductions on an assembly line. The Bible wasn't written to change us into cookie-cutter Christians or paper doll saints. On the contrary, the folks I read about in the Book are as different as Rahab and Esther: one a former prostitute and the other a Queen . . . as unusual as Amos and Stephen, fig-picker turned prophet and deacon who became a martyr. Variety honours God, predictability and mediocrity bore Him. Take a look down the long hall of fame in church history. Some of those folk would never have been welcome in most evangelical churches today . . . 'Too extreme . . . too eccentric . . . too liberal!'

God has made each one of us as we are. He is hard at work shaping us into the image He has in mind. His only pattern (for character) is His Son. He wants each one of us to be unique . . . an individual blend and expression unlike any other person. There is only one you. There is only one me. Grace finds pleasure in differences, encourages individuality, smiles on variety and leaves plenty of room for disagreement . . . [21]

This is an important point, because some of our 'bad guilt' feelings come directly from the atmosphere in our churches. The fact that some men feel guilty about having their hair in a pony-tail or wearing an ear-ring may have little to do with the Holy Spirit and more to do with the unspoken and spoken attempts of the Church to make them fit into some kind of bland 'Christian' image. How many have been lost because the Church tried to dress them in a uniform that only chafed and irritated? God is not on a crusade to turn you into someone other than who you are. He made you.

Extra-biblical rules

Grace-killing churches love to wave Bibles around but, ironically for them, Scripture isn't enough. They are unwilling to trust holy Scripture and the Holy Spirit, so they come up with lists of extra rules and regulations that have no basis in anything God has ever actually said. These rules and regulations are often strange and inconsistent. I have been to churches where to go to the cinema is wrong, but renting a video is fine. Some churches sell books on Sundays but, because they don't believe in trading on the Sabbath, people pay for their books at the church office on Monday. One place in Texas forbids its women to shave their legs!

If this appears odd, remember it's nothing new. Religion and rules seem to go together. It seems that in their desire to stop people from falling into sin, the religious are drawn to rules and regulations like iron filings to a magnet. In New Testament times the Pharisees had rules about how much you should greet a bride on her wedding day, or how much you should comfort a widow at her husband's funeral. They had a rule that forbade you to look in a mirror on the Sabbath, because you might just spot a stray grey hair and, if you pulled it out, you would be guilty of working on God's day of rest! (For Jesus' criticism of their excessive legalism, see Matthew 23 and Mark 7:5–13.) In the early days of the Church, Paul had to be firm with the Christians at Colosse about moving away from the old rules on what you could eat and drink (Col. 2:6–23).

Tears that never dry

We gathered in the minister's study a few minutes before the meeting was due to start. Everyone looked pristine and prepared in immaculate suits, but the atmosphere was light-hearted and warm – until the moment the pastor suggested we join hands in a small circle and pray that God would show up at the service. In the space of a few seconds, men who had been happy and smiling were choked with emotion. They wept and wailed, sobbing, begging and pleading, in soul-wrenching travail. Then, as soon as someone said 'Amen', they were all happy again. I was mystified.

And then I realised. This group of Christians had decided that the only way to approach God was with tears and apology. Maybe this is why so-called 'holy laughter' causes such a stir among some churches. Many Christians seem to feel that tears and sadness, or even pomp and solemnity, are more appropriate in God's presence than laughter and joy. For years they sang songs about joy . . .

> 'I've got this joy, joy, joy, joy, down in my heart!'
> (Everyone shouts, 'Where?!')
> 'Down in my heart!' ('Where?!')
> 'Down in my heart!'

Sadly, that mystical, never-to-be-expressed joy is so deeply buried in the unreachable caverns of our hearts that it would probably take a nuclear explosion to bring any of it to the surface. Perhaps this is one of the reasons for so-called 'holy laughter.' Some people need a major encounter with the Spirit of God to enable them to laugh in a Christian meeting.

Of course, there is a time to weep, and we should find ourselves stirred and angered by the sickening images of oppression and injustice that appear daily on our television screens. And there is a time to laugh. Occasionally people get very upset about my sense of humour. I got this letter at the close of one meeting

> Sir, we would see Jesus, not your comedy act and non-sensical gibberish. You can't win souls to Jesus with all that nonsense. You are not a preacher, you are a comedian. You have missed your calling.

The note was unsigned, anonymous venom. But it convinced me all the more of the need to see Christians relax and have fun. Still, I can't pretend to enjoy it when those who are nervous of fun criticise me. I went to God about this one day and asked him, 'Lord, have you called me to be a fool for you?', expecting an extended and lengthy answer.

He was brief and to the point: 'Yes.'

Disconnected from reality

Most church services provide a dose of sacred theatre. Atmospheres are carefully created by stirring music and eloquent oratory. Mix it all together with a sense of the ceremonial and perhaps some wonderful architecture, and you have an other-worldly effect, designed to encourage us to lift our eyes from the mundane domestication of life and focus on the eternal, heavenly realities of the living God. Fine. Carefully chosen, well-played music and a beautifully prepared service can be very helpful aids to worship. But we must hold in tension the fact that real life doesn't come backed by a romantic soundtrack.

A lot of guilt may be generated because we don't have the same feelings about God on Monday as we do on Sunday. Sometimes this guilt arises because the diet of teaching in our church isn't related enough to everyday experience. The vicar's twenty-five part expository series entitled 'Inside the gall bladders of Leviticus – an exegetical overview' may be a stunning piece of sermonising craftsmanship, but it's not likely to connect with the realities of life in the twenty-first century. I find this particularly true when it comes to issues of sex and sexuality, surely a minefield of potential shame for many of us.

I can remember feeling guilty as a young Christian because my awareness as an adolescent that I was a sexual being seemed quite inappropriate in the light of the church's sanitised teaching on holiness. A Baptist minister in our town suffered great criticism because he dared to use the term 'love-making' from the pulpit. Thankfully, in our church we had the annual obligatory chat about sex from the youth leader, a jolly chap, but you really needed a dictionary and a map reference to know what on earth he was on about. In a way things have not moved on much since the medieval church taught that the Holy Spirit swiftly vacated the marital bedroom during sexual intercourse and then returned when all was safely concluded.

This conspiracy of silence about human intimacy creates a sense of guilt which makes our sexuality – such a powerful part of all of us – somehow irrelevant and perhaps unseemly for the 'good' Christian. The fact that we feel shame when we acknowledge struggles with our sexuality has more to do with a prudish Church than a prudish God, who designed sex in marriage to be fun and not just procreative!

Problems of guilt also arise when churches are led by outgoing, confident Type A personalities who make others feel that in order to be effective followers of Jesus, they have to be loud extroverts too. Donald Sloat reflects on what it can feel like to listen to a dynamic Christian speaker

> Guiltily, I wondered what was wrong with me. Somehow the Christian life had never been as automatic or thrilling for me. Mine was more of a struggle . . . in retrospect, I realised that some people are naturally emotional, easily excited about anything, whether it be Christ or a used car. In other words, a definite part

of the speaker's meaningful salvation experience was due to his particular personality style. But in his well-intentioned enthusiasm to share his experience, he implied that everyone ought to feel the same way that he did.

Disconnected from usefulness

Grace-killing churches can quickly become little more than a group of sincerely pious individuals whose mission in life is focused on staying as 'free from sin' as they can because Jesus' Second Coming is anticipated at any moment. They seem inevitably to lose their evangelistic thrust: evangelism means having sinful, undisciplined, inappropriately dressed and inappropriately behaved people in church with us who don't look like us, sound like us or do the things we do. Trying to be a church with people who are different can be uncomfortable; better avoid it all together. Soon the absence of new converts leads a church to becoming socially and culturally irrelevant, and – hey presto – you have a holy ghetto.

Holy ghettoes can lead to two outcomes. In one, the church becomes so smug about their 'purity' that they start to shun the rest of us who, in their eyes, will never be acceptable to God. Or week in, week out, a morality-holiness agenda is preached, drumming into church members the message of their own unworthiness. Deeply sincere people who really do want to love and serve God are forced to walk to the front, week in, week out, to let their God know yet again that they just aren't good enough. We shouldn't be surprised to discover that evangelical Christians consistently rate the lowest in self-esteem profiles.

In either instance, the result is a church disconnected from reality and of no earthly use to anyone. Holy ghettoes

tend not to be involved in social action or community programmes: they are either unwilling – that is, not convicted
enough – to do anything to help others or they are so preoccupied with their shortcomings – tottering under the
burden of condemnation – that they are paralysed by guilt.
Then, as the people of God get ever more weary, they lose
any kind of motivation to share their faith with the rest of
the world. Tragically, it's probably for the best, because the
world doesn't need to be converted to a life filled with
shame.

But it doesn't have to be that way. I am so grateful to
that first family of mine which, with handshakes and
hugs, welcomed me to faith. I came out of that counselling room thrilled by the wonderful news of the
gospel, but very aware that I couldn't see, touch or feel
this God of love. That line-up of very seeable, touchable
people served to drive home the truth of my relationship
with God, which for a while I could enjoy without fear
or question. I was loved. No wonder I fell for the church
that night. The love affair continues to this day.

Chapter 6

The restoration of a shame addict: part 1

'Get away from me, Lord – I'm a sinner.'

Peter. A supernatural surfer, striding impossibly across the waves towards Jesus, until sinking doubt pulled him under (Matt. 14:25–31). Chained hand and foot, he sleeps peacefully on Death Row, until an angel stirs him with a slap and leads him quickly to freedom (Acts 12:1–17).

Peter. Healing pulsates from his shadow as he strolls around Jerusalem. Not much silver and gold in his pocket, but the power of life and death is in his hands (Acts 3:1–10). Fearless prophet on the day of Pentecost, standing up with his friends and giving the religious movers and shakers some serious in-your-face confrontation (Acts 2:14–41). Key player in the early days of the Christian church.

Peter. A man struggling with a toxic capacity for guilt. A shame addict.

Shame addicts are people-pleasers. Unable to feel secure in their friendships, they are convinced no one could really love them if they knew their full story. So they spend their lives trying to accommodate, to help: anything to appear trustworthy. They want to go with the flow because they are desperate for the crowd to approve of them. They even hunger for approval from total strangers.

Look at that man over there (John 18:25–27). He warms his hands in the fire, but seems eager to stay in the shadows. A servant girl passes by and seems to recognise him. His eyes are dead and cold as, with an explosion of swear words, he protests mistaken identity and rubbishes not just the last few years of his life but the One who has filled all his waking moments. He is running scared and doesn't want to stand out.

Look at that man over there (Gal. 2:11–21). He puts his head down and crosses the street as a Gentile approaches. This is Antioch, some fifteen years after Jesus' resurrection, and Peter has been hanging out with the Gentiles – until the religious crew gets wind of it and tongues start wagging. So Peter decides to deny his friends once again and resign from the luncheon club. He wants to please, to fit in, and he almost gets away with it – until Paul turns up with an icy blast about hypocrisy.

Shame addicts find it almost impossible to acknowledge that they might just fail. They have to get it right every time. Jesus lets Peter know that there are some pitfalls ahead (Matt. 26:31–35). Denial is coming, three-time treachery, and the cock is going to crow over that dark dawn. And the man who wants to please refuses to believe it. Two and two will equal five before he would mess up. No – even if the whole world runs, Jesus, you can count on me. Failure? It's not in my vocabulary.

Look at that man on the lake (Luke 5:1–8). He and his fishing partners have had a rough night, working till dawn in the hope of a catch. But the nets are empty. The sun comes up and with it that sweeping fatigue which cannot even find comfort in a feeling of mission accomplished. Then Jesus charters Peter's boat and uses it as a pulpit to preach from. And when he has finished his sermon, he decides to go fishing. Ignoring the fishermen's professional pride, this carpenter's Son issues some strange instructions: 'Put the nets out there – in the deep water.'

Peter's mind screams in protest. Everybody knows you don't fish in deep water during the day. No, you head for the shallows and try to scoop the feeding shoals that skitter around the surface. That's the wrong place for a catch, Jesus, and this is the wrong time. We should know because we (the experts?) have been at this all night and there's nothing in our nets to show for it.

However, with a shrug of his shoulders and vague hope in his heart, Peter does as he's told. The nets go over the side. The descending rope runs quickly through his hardened fingers, disappearing into the deep. Wiping sweat from his brow and shielding his eyes against the glare on the waves, he waits, they all wait, in silence.

Suddenly, the ropes jump, lurch and snap tight in Peter's hands. The bow tilts sharply as, far below, fish hurl themselves into the nets. Whooping and yelling for help, Peter begins to pull up the biggest catch of his life.

The nets jerk and drop under the strain as rope twine gives way to the sheer weight of the catch. The front of the boat dips dangerously beneath the surface. Peter shouts to his friends and partners, who hastily manoeuvre their boats and grab at the edges of nets. Bring it up quickly before we lose the lot!

At last, the impossibly bulging nets surface, dripping and sagging with countless teeming, flailing fish, their silvery bodies slapping in the sunlight. The men begin to scoop the fish out of the heaving morass and into their boats as quickly as possible, their laughter and shouts echoing across the water. This is something they will tell their children and their children's children.

Peter looks around, taking in this bizarre sight – boats crammed full of fish and sinking in the surf.

Something snaps in his mind. In a second his joy and astonishment evaporate as a deep shadow of shame drapes itself across his soul. Throwing himself down onto a floor awash with foaming sea and flapping fish, he grabs Jesus' knees and sobs a desperate request: 'Go away from me, Lord – I am a sinful man.'

Sinful man?

What sin had Peter committed during this brief voyage to make him want Jesus to leave?

The fact is, Peter wasn't simply feeling bad about a specific act of wrongdoing: he was drowning in a sea of shame, his sinful nature naked and shivering in the presence of Jesus' purity. But why should he have such a shame attack? It has been suggested that three circumstances conspired together to produce it. Before we rush to see how Jesus helped Peter recover, let's observe his shame for a moment longer.

Small failures trigger big shame

The fishing trip had been a washout before Jesus decided to join it. Peter was no hobby angler. As a commercial fisherman, he had found himself, after a hard day's night, with nothing to take to market. He was a family man, but there was no catch to take home to feed his loved ones. He had nothing but frustration, a heavy heart and aching joints. The emphasis of the biblical text echoes his weariness: 'Master, we have worked hard all night and haven't caught anything.' Peter had failed to deliver in an area where he was supposed to be an expert. So he slapped a label on his own forehead: in black felt-tip (or a reed pen dripping with ink), he scrawled 'Sinner.' This independent, self-assured man became aware that he just wasn't good enough compared to the greatness and the beauty of this strange Teacher, who seemed to know all there was to know about fishing.

It has been said that shame is like a spider's web: jiggle just one corner of it and the whole thing begins to shake furiously. Perhaps Peter's fishing failure reminded him of a thousand and one other shortcomings, impurities, false motives, lusts, fears. One moment of failure touched all of his deep shame. So the words that tumbled out of his mouth speak not so much of concern at a specific sin or two, but rather an all-embracing awareness of his sinful nature. No wonder he was in such agony; to go to God for forgiveness for a single sin may be relatively easy: we confess, name the sin and receive specific forgiveness. But how do we go to the cross with our entire being? How do we confess who and what we are, and receive relief? After we have admitted our sinful nature, we still have it. We can't shrug it off once and for all. Which of us, having taken even a brief look inside ourselves, has not been horrified, overwhelmed, by the knowledge that we just don't care enough, give enough, love enough, pray enough – and ten thousand other 'enoughs'?

Overwhelmed by the one who sees everything

Peter has spent at least eight or nine cold, back-breaking hours searching the inky waters for a catch, and here comes Jesus who can see fish where they shouldn't have been. As he peers down into the depths, he is jolted by the realisation that Jesus can see things no one else can. His eyesight extends right down deep, where the sunlight has faded and there are only dark shadows. If Jesus can see the unseeable in water; what would he see in Peter's soul?

If you feel at home with God, the fact that he sees everything can be comforting: 'O Lord, you have searched me and you know me . . . Such knowledge is too wonderful for me' (Ps. 139:1,6). However; if shame lurks within you, the all-seeing eye of God becomes an unwelcome camera which barges through layer after layer of defences, threatening to bare your naked soul.

Once there was a man who wanted to kill God. This man was a writer; so he created a story with a character who assassinated God. When asked why he did such a thing, the man said that it just had to be done, because God knew far too much: 'He saw with eyes that saw everything . . . all my concealed disgrace and ugliness . . . He crawled into my dirtiest nooks. This most curious one had to die.'

The man's name was Friedrich Nietzsche. His father was a Lutheran minister, but young Friedrich preached another creed: God is dead. Believing that love and mercy were worthless and that power was everything, desperate to silence God's voice and blind God's eyes, Nietzsche declared war on heaven. Let God die, and bury guilt with him.

Peter didn't want Jesus to die, but he did want Jesus to go: Jesus knew far too much.

Overwhelmed by the gift Jesus gave him

Fish. Hundreds, maybe thousands of them. Not just 'enough' in some measured, rationed kind of way, enough to give Peter and his friends a good day at the market and a marvellous supper at home. A bumper, over-the-top catch.

Why did Jesus give Peter such a haul? Simple. He loved Peter and wanted to do something wonderfully relevant to help him. The love burning in his heart for the worn-out fisherman wasn't some remote, generalised affection, but a determined kindness that desired to help. It was love that Peter hadn't earned or worked for, that he didn't deserve. And because he didn't deserve it, he couldn't accept it. Instead, he felt the need to run from this bumper catch, this bumper love. Like Adam and Eve who went scurrying into the undergrowth when they heard the footsteps of God, like Felix who covered his ears to shut Paul out when the preaching got too up close and personal (Acts 24:24–25), Peter felt compelled to do just about anything to escape from this all-seeing, all-loving Man.

Stop and consider the bulging gift from God to you. The writer to the Hebrews calls it 'such a great salvation'. John, writing in his Gospel, searches for adequate words to declare the enormity of God's love. I'll paraphrase his words because they are so familiar: 'You want to know just how great God's love is for you and for the world? Well, I'll tell you how to measure it: he gave his own one and only Son to die for you – that's the size of it' (John 3:16).

The apostle Paul struggles with the big God and his big love, and prays that his friends in Ephesus will be able to fathom the unfathomable: 'I pray that you, being rooted and established in love, may have power . . . to grasp how wide and long and high and deep is the love of Christ, and to know this love that surpasses knowledge . . .' (Eph 3:17–18).

'How great is the love the Father has lavished on us, that we should be called children of God . . . and that is what we are!' (1 John 3:1).

Overwhelmed by the unique Jesus

Nearly three whirlwind years later, Peter has learned that when you hang around with Jesus, absolutely anything is possible. He disrupts funerals: at Nain, a weeping widow watches in stunned amazement as her dead son climbs out of his makeshift coffin. At Bethany, a stinking Lazarus, hands and feet still trussed in foul grave clothes, struggles out of his tomb at Jesus' command, and joins his family for lunch. Demons evacuate their human captives with a scream, their days of tormenting their victims over. Crazy people find their minds. The blind find their sight. When the wine runs dry at a wedding reception, with a few gallons of water and a couple of co-operative servants, Jesus produces the best wine anyone has ever tasted, saving both the celebration and the good name of the host.

Those remarkable months make Peter aware that Jesus is, in a sense, 'his own man'. Certainly Jesus steadfastly refuses to allow anyone to divert him from his mission, even though there are many who want to hijack him from his calling. Jesus lives to one agenda – to carry out the will of his Father. But still they try . . .

The Zealots want him to be the Messiah king who will overthrow Israel's Roman oppressors. The devil wants him to have the whole world – in exchange for his soul. The Pharisees try to force him into religious conformity. Even the disciples want him to be their highway to heavenly privilege. Give us high flying thrones in your future kingdom, please, Jesus. Torch those people over there, please, Jesus. Send these hungry people away, please, Jesus. Don't waste time hugging and blessing kids when you should be debating theology with the Pharisees (Mark 10:35–45; Luke 9:51–56; Matt. 14:15; 19:13–15). Peter too tries to 'adjust' Jesus. The prospect of Christ walking towards a cross appals him. He tells Jesus that it's a bad plan – and receives a stinging rebuke for his trouble (Matt. 16:21–23).

One of the most poignant examples of Peter's attempts to 'adjust Jesus' occurs in John 13:1–17. The Master has stripped down and wrapped himself in a towel, and is busily cleaning the sand and dirt from between his disciples' toes, a bowl of greying water at his knees. This is too much for Peter. How can this Lord who speaks to the elements, who heals people, who terrifies demons, who challenges death, stoop to become this humble, this kind, this caring? Peter refuses to allow Jesus to wash his feet. But once again he is put in his place: 'Either I wash your feet – or we have no future together.' Jesus simply won't surrender to Peter's pride, Peter's stereotypes, Peter's protests. He is going to be just who he is – wonderful, kind, spontaneous, risk-taking, a Servant King. In short, Jesus will be Jesus.

I'm reminded of the man who clashed with me during a debate on alcohol consumption. I asked him what he thought about Jesus turning water into wine. He dropped his eyes, shook his head sadly and said 'I really wish he hadn't done that.' Jesus frustrates us by his refusal to act according to our 'stained-glass' ideas of him.

The first step towards healing our shame is to rediscover the real Jesus. If we want to be free, we must allow him to be his true, wonderful, gracious self. Our pride wants to put a mask on his face and make him our employer, our Master, our Lord – but not our gracious forgiver. We moan about his willingness to wash our smelly feet and perform a host of other services in areas that we are ashamed of. John the Baptist was right (John 1:29): the first step for sinners is to look again at the Lamb of God who takes away the sins of the world. And in his letter to a group of Christians who were straying from the work of Christ and returning to man-made systems of sacrifice, the unknown author writes: 'Let us fix our eyes on Jesus, the author and perfecter of our faith, who for the joy set before him endured the cross, scorning its shame, and sat down at the right hand of the throne of God' (Heb. 12:2).

Salvation begins and ends with Jesus, the Alpha and the Omega. Look at him, his face locked in the agony of dying, gasping out those final bloody bubbles of air for us. He refuses to be anything other than our Saviour.

Look at him bearing the awfulness of our shame as he despises it and triumphs over it.

Look at him reigning in authority, seated at the Father's side. He refuses to be anything other than our ruling, redeeming Lord.

Our 'walking backwards' ends not as we turn to gaze upon some false mirage of our own goodness; rather, as sinners, it ends as we look on the One who dealt with sin at the cross. Don't hide your eyes from the brightness. Don't run from the remarkable spectacle of him exposed in bloody nakedness so that we can be forgiven. Turn round and simply look at the *real* Jesus. It is here that healing begins.

Chapter 7

The restoration of a shame addict: part 2

'Anyone for breakfast?'
Jesus is alive. So what?

To make such a statement seems almost blasphemous, but I think Peter may well have gone through a phase in his life when he felt just that way. These dark days are described at the end of John's Gospel (chapter 21). Peter has been on an emotional roller-coaster for days. The arrest and trial of his best friend. The sickening denial and the crowing rooster. The blood, sweat and tears of the crucifixion. While Peter stands helpless at a distance, every blow, every jeer from the crowd is an echo of his own denial. Then, when everything seems lost, comes the explosion of the resurrection, the empty tomb. Jesus strolls through walls into rooms where the doors and windows have been locked and barred.

But even a resurrection doesn't guarantee joy. Peter still lives with the unresolved shadow of his guilt. His denial sticks into his side like a sharp goad, and once again the shame addict wants to fade into the background. He decides to return to safe, familiar territory

– fishing. He is on the run, make no mistake. Some commentators have interpreted the statement 'I'm going out to fish' to mean literally 'I'm going to sink out of sight.' The other disciples don't have much to say to help him. Their answer mirrors their own confusion: 'We'll go with you.' The inaugural session of the Naffed-off Community Church is in session.

This episode is a repeat of Luke 5. Peter wants to get away. He catches nothing in the process. A cold, back-breaking night's work ends with nothing but empty nets. A stranger appears on the shore and shouts a risky question across the water: 'Haven't you any fish?'

Such a question would hardly be welcomed by a group of failed fishing experts. It's probably a miracle that Peter didn't respond with 'No, pal – and you haven't got any black eyes yet either.'

But there's another bumper catch, followed by an invitation to breakfast, and Peter goes for a swim. By the end of the morning, the shame addict has taken some serious steps towards resolution and wholeness. It was the greatest breakfast of his life. Let's look carefully at how Jesus helps Peter turn round and end his days of walking backwards for good.

Nice to see you

If I had been in charge of the arrangements for Christ's post-resurrection appearances, I would have gone in for some flashy, unforgettable choreography. A chorus line of fluorescent angels tap-dancing on a golden sandy beach. The London Symphony Orchestra playing the prophetic version of Handel's *Messiah* (prophetic because it hadn't been written yet) with a ten-thousand-voice choir. The Royal Albert Hall organ erected especially on the beach and booming away. Cascades of fireworks zigzagging in pinks and yellows and greens, turning the grey dawn sky into a Technicolor backcloth.

But Jesus isn't into flash and splash. If anything, he seems most keen on quiet understatement. He shows up in the garden and Mary mistakes him for the gardener (John 20:14–16). He strolls along the Emmaus road with a couple of friends, and they only recognise him over a meal at their place (Luke 24:13–35). The disciples have no clue as to the identity of the stranger yelling at them from the shoreline. But then he says something that begins to trigger all kinds of memories: 'Throw your net on the right side of the boat.' That voice is familiar, and so is the advice. Nearly three years ago, didn't Jesus say . . .? Might as well give it a go . . .

Then the three-year-old miracle is repeated. Nets come up bursting with fish, so much so that they can't land them.

Same strategy. Same success. Same voice. John rubs his tired eyes as he peers across the water – and identifies the stranger. Typical of John. He always understands before Peter, and Peter always leaps into action before John.

Jesus comes in an unexpected manner and at an unexpected time. Peter is in a trough of shame-generated depression. He doesn't 'feel' spiritual. But as Adrian Plass said in a passing comment to me some while ago, 'Feelings are not a barometer of the love of God for me today.' We charismatics often tend to measure the level of activity in our lives according to how we feel. The truth is, though Peter feels hideous, God is quietly at work. And how he works.

Look at the man on the beach. He paces the sand, his fists clenching and unclenching, his face a mask of anger and frustration, his eyes burning with indignation.

If I've told them once, I've told them a thousand times. I appointed them to become fishers of *men*. I told them what was going to happen. Arrest. Trial. Death. Life again. I've done all I can to assure them of my love and the life of eternity I can give them. And now look! The idiots are out on the waters again, back to what they were before I ever walked into their lives, apparently ignorant of everything I've told them over the last thirty-six months. And no catch as well – pathetic. Peter! James! John! The rest of you too! Get those sad, empty nets out of the water and get yourselves onto the beach, here, *now*. We need to talk . . .

But it wasn't like that.

Look at Jesus on the beach. According to some commentators, the Greek translation says, 'With pleasure he stood there.' He calls out to them, 'Friends, haven't you any fish?'

Friends. A nice, safe word, but somewhat 'churchy.' One can almost imagine a buck-toothed vicar with a sickly smile and a sad lisp . . . 'Good morning, friends.' However; some commentators suggest that the word Jesus uses is not 'friends' but the Greek word *paedion* meaning boys or children.' (A modern derivative is our word 'paediatrician', someone who cares for children.) 'Hey, lads! No fish, eh?'

To the guilty, Jesus comes quietly, gently, with an invitation to turn away from vain labouring and to rest with him for a while. If we are to discover the Jesus who can heal our guilt, we need to learn how to 'breakfast' with Jesus: that is, to put aside some time for thinking and quiet reflection. Those who rush through life attending only to external demands, never giving attention to the health of their inner spirit, will never find relief from shame. Jesus doesn't come crashing in with a quick 'zap' to lift us up from the mire of guilt. We meet him as we deliberately look for him. Thomas Kelly says 'God never guides us into an intolerable scramble of panting feverishness.'

Time for reality

John's yell of excitement echoes across the waves: 'It is the Lord!' Peter doesn't need another invitation. Forget the fish, forget his fears – let's just get to where Jesus is. He has got to talk to him. Only he does something a little strange: he puts his coat on before going for a swim.

Now I've had people offer all kinds of explanations for this bizarre behaviour. ('I think I'll go for a swim. Now where did I put my coat . . .?') Allow me to speculate on this one. It may well be that there will come a time when I stand before God and he says, 'Jeff, that stuff you said about Peter and his coat – it was all a load of rot.' But consider this possibility anyway.

Peter instinctively tries to cover himself, to hide from what he perceives to be the glare of Jesus' piercing eyes. As he leaps overboard, he instinctively grabs his cloak, even though it will slow him down and become waterlogged and heavy. He was delighted to see Jesus, but painfully aware of his denial which had not, as far as we know, been discussed at all until this point. Lingering shame lurked in his soul, so he gets dressed up for a swim.

But hiding behind unreality can't survive when Jesus is around. As Peter splashes his way up the beach, the first thing he sees isn't Jesus but a charcoal fire with bread and fish on the coals. Jesus has already been fishing. And a charcoal fire.

Now where did Peter deny Jesus? While warming his hands at a charcoal fire (John 18:18).

'Great to see you, Lord. How's it going?' Peter charges up the beach. Or is it possible he says something else to Jesus before the other disciples join them – something about being sorry, something Peter didn't want anyone else to hear?

The disciples join them and they all sit down.

Then the questions begin: 'Do you love me?' Jesus doesn't delve into the circumstances of the denial: he is interested in the root of Peter's problem. He chooses to use the Greek word *agapetos* – this refers to the highest form of sacrificial, selfless love. Peter feels like a dwarf in the face of such a question and doesn't even try to bluff his way through. He wants Jesus to know that, yes, he does love him, but it's a *phileo*-type of love, the lesser love of friendship.

Again Jesus pops the big question; again Peter won't budge from reality: 'No, Lord, not *agape* – *phileo*.'

The third time, the knife cuts Peter to the quick. 'Peter was hurt because Jesus asked him the third time, "Do you love me?" He said, "Lord, you know all things; you know that I love you"' (John 21:17). Jesus changes the word: 'Do you love (*phileo*) me?'

Peter gives up. Jesus knew where the fish were three years ago. Jesus knew where the fish were today. 'Lord, you know all things, you know that I love you.' Once so quick to cover up his imperfections, Peter has broken through into a place of reality. He refuses to offer cheap, meaningless explanations, to rationalise or excuse himself.

If we are to deal with guilt, whether it be true or false, we need not to fight but to surrender. Yes, we are sinners. We can't do anything except accept the helping hand of God. We don't have to try to stammer out our excuses – just agree with the damning facts: we have messed up and that's that. Relief comes in our nakedness before

God, in the realisation that he knows everything there is to know about us, but is still pleased to see us *and enjoys our company*. Let the Accuser say that we have sinned – we have!

And it isn't enough to be real with God: we also need to be real with one another. Satan loves to work in darkness where secrecy permeates the atmosphere. There is a tragic irony when we say that we are part of the family of God and yet continue to struggle alone with our sins. We say that we 'attend church' – as if the sum total of 'church' can be expressed in what happens in a particular building on a Sunday morning.

'Hello, brother (helpful term if you don't know the person's name). How are you?'

'Fine, praise the Lord. And you . . . er . . . brother?'

'Wonderful! See you next week.' (Encounter ends, singing begins.)

Gordon MacDonald, author of the classic *Ordering your Private World*, went through a twilight period when his private world imploded due to his making sinful, disastrous choices. He fell into immorality. During that time of shadowy compromise, he learned how to pretend, and in the process he bumped into a whole lot of other 'pretenders' in the church. He remarked sadly, 'Pretending is the common cold of evangelicalism.'

Thankfully, we know that MacDonald made the good decision to step into the light and to submit himself to a process of reorientation. Today his ministry is full of anointing and inspiration – a testimony of grace. But the pretence he encountered is a million miles from what God intends for his people. We haven't been called to shallow Christian friendships based on religious posturing. We have the opportunity to embrace authentic kingdom relationships – strong, resilient, founded on truth and love. 'Fellowship' is a familiar word in Christian circles; it means 'partnership.' True fellowship can only take place when honesty and reality are also present.

> If we walk in the light, as he is in the light, [then] we have fellowship with one another, and the blood of Jesus, his Son, purifies us from all sin (1 John 1:7)

John is teaching two vital facts about fellowship. First, fellowship is impossible without reality. If I pretend when I'm around you, we may have some kind of vague human interaction, but it certainly isn't fellowship. Of course we can't be totally open with everyone we meet – and neither should we be! When people ask us the standard British question, 'How are you?', they probably don't want us to whip out a report, complete with X-Ray charts and medical records. But we can commit ourselves to being totally transparent with trusted friends, taking the time to share with them the secrets of our souls. As we do, we break the power that those secrets have over us. Light floods into our hearts as we stand, open and real, before one another.

What a refreshing thing it is to be known! Gerald Coates has observed, 'There are people who know everything that there is to know about me – and I can't tell you what a relief it is.' It is humbling too.

> Confession in the presence of a brother is the profoundest kind of humiliation. It hurts, it cuts a man down, it is a dreadful blow to the pride. To stand there before a brother as a sinner is an ignominy that is almost unbearable. In the confession of concrete sins, the old man dies a painful, shameful death before the eyes of his brother. As long as I am by myself in the confession of my sins everything remains in the dark, but in the presence of a brother the sin has to be brought into the light.[23]

John is also emphasising the link between real fellow-ship and our ability to receive forgiveness. Protestants have rejected ecclesiastical confession, where an 'ordained priest' has some kind of church-bestowed authority to grant absolution. However, in affirming the priesthood of all believers, I feel that we have rejected all forms of confession. There is something very power-ful in being able to share your struggles with a friend, who can then assure you of the love and forgiveness of God, not as part of a ritual but as a fellow disciple of Christ.

'God has given us our brothers and sisters to stand in Christ's stead and make God's presence and forgiveness real to us' wrote Richard Foster. Perhaps if we had a revival of reality, we would have a revival of power in the church. Certainly that's the impression I get when I look at the epistle of James. Read these verses and breathe the fresh air of real friendship

> Is any one of you in trouble? He should pray. Is anyone happy? Let him sing songs of praise. Is any one of you sick? He should call the elders of the church to pray over him and anoint him with oil in the name of the Lord. And the prayer offered in faith will make the sick person well; the Lord will raise him up. If he has sinned, he will be forgiven. Therefore confess your sins to each other and pray for each other so that you may be healed. (Jas. 5:13–16)

The Amplified Version is helpful

> Confess to one another therefore your faults – your slips, your false steps, your offences, your sins; and pray for one another, that you may be healed and restored to a spiritual tone of mind and heart.

Jim Bakker, the disgraced 'PTL' televangelist, sacrificed his integrity for a brief twenty-minute sexual encounter. Overwhelmed by guilt and shame, he went to a friend and counsellor

> My friend knew that the only way I would find emo-
> tional health and spiritual freedom was by seeking for-
> giveness from God, forgiveness from Jessica Hahn [with
> whom he had had the affair] and forgiveness from
> myself. Together, the counsellor and I knelt down on the
> floor and began to pray. I cried out to God for forgive-
> ness. I literally lay face down on the floor; prostrate
> before God. Then, in a sense, the counsellor placed him-
> self in the position of a priest to me and declared, 'Now
> I tell you before God, Jim Bakker, that you have been for-
> given of God.'[24]

This is the radical nature of God's radical kingdom.

John the Baptist is ducking repentant sinners in the River Jordan. Before they are plunged beneath the waves, a public confession of sin takes place. God's kingdom was coming, so John introduces the people to repentant reality (Matt. 3:1–6). Revival hits the occult-bound city of Ephesus. The citizens confess their sins and hold a public book-burning. The kingdom has come to their city (Acts 19:18–20).

So much of the agony of walking backwards is caused by our insistence that we suffer in secret. In the solitude of our minds, our thoughts run riot in a tangle of private confusion. When we throw open the cupboard and allow light to shine on the skeletons tucked away in there, this light will overcome the darkness as we reass-
ure one another of the truth. Reality dawns, and our confusion is shattered.

Love that whispers, love that shouts

Fish, for Peter a symbol of Jesus' kindness and generosity. Bread, just like the bread Jesus broke that last evening before the terrible day: 'This is my body, broken for you.' And now Jesus' hands are moving quickly across the coals, adjusting the fish and the bread, and his hands have holes in them.

Perhaps Jesus, who loved using signs and symbols to communicate his message, was speaking to Peter through that charcoal fire: yes, you have sinned, but my gift is enough to cover the coals of your failure.

God seems to love using prophetic drama to get his message of forgiveness across. He whispers this message in the drama of communion (his body broken and his blood shed for our sins) and baptism (the death of the self and new life in God). He shouts his message in the drama of circumcision (Josh. 5:7–9), a sharp (literally) reminder to the people of Israel that they were more than just a bedraggled group of exiles – they were his people. 'Today I have rolled away the reproach of Egypt from you' – this was a shout of mercy signalling a new beginning, but the people needed the agony of the knife to let them know that this was really so.

I was speaking at Spring Harvest one year, and Gary, the drummer in the worship band, walked up to the microphone and calmly announced that God had told him there was someone in the crowd who had had an abortion some years earlier. This person had genuinely sought God's forgiveness, but had been unable to find peace and freedom. Gary said that God had told him the day, month and year this abortion had taken place as a sign to the person they really were forgiven.

At the end of the meeting, a young woman came forward for private prayer, shattered, thrilled, blessed and overwhelmed by the God who wanted her to know peace and forgiveness so much that he was prepared to shout at her in order to make it happen.

Sometimes Christians get very worked up as they seek to discover the will of God for their lives. One thing is certain: it is the will of God for each one of us to know that Christ's work on the cross is big enough to cover our sins – whether God whispers or shouts it.

Accept the judge's final verdict

Peter had seen himself as a useless failure, but Jesus delivered a different verdict on his case: yes, he saw Peter as a failure, but a forgiven one. Rejection was never in Jesus' mind; restoration was his plan. He didn't think of punishing Peter either. Shocking as it may seem, God doesn't punish his children: rather, he disciplines them as a loving parent, because he cares for us.

Many Christians live in fear that God will punish them – lightning will strike them, or one of their children is going to die – because of some past sin. But 'there is no fear in love. But perfect love drives out fear, because fear has to do with punishment. The one who fears is not made perfect in love' (1 John 4:18).

Peter had to submit to Jesus' love and begin to see himself as Jesus saw him. Here's the bottom line. Accepting God's forgiveness is a matter of simple obedience. If he declares us clean, who are we to argue? So often we happily submit to God when he gives us a command that involves sacrifice or pain. It makes us feel good to pay a price to follow Jesus. But when he gives us days of fun, laughter or prosperity – when he delivers his considered verdict and demands that we accept we are forgiven – we feel that we have the right to struggle and protest. Again, who are we to fight with God?

Psychologist John White describes a counselling session with a man called Howard, who had been diagnosed as suffering from psychotic depression.

> One day, we were discussing forgiveness. Howard said, 'I want it so bad . . . but I'm too bad for that, I don't deserve ever to be forgiven.' I replied, 'You're darn right you don't.' I felt my anger increasing. 'And who do you think you are to say Christ's death was not enough for you? Who are you to feel you must add your miserable pittance to the great gift God offers you? Is his sacrifice not good enough for the likes of you?'
>
> Suddenly Howard began both to cry and to pray at once . . .
>
> 'God, I'm really sorry. I didn't mean to offend you . . . I don't know how to say it . . . thank you, God, thank you.'[25]

Refusing to accept God's forgiveness isn't holy, pious or pleasing to him. It's ungrateful, offensive rebellion that shows a faulty understanding of God. People know their own sinfulness so well: what they need to know much more is the extent of God's love and his willingness to forgive. So, stop arguing!

Peter had to learn not to argue with Jesus. He had tried it a number of times, as we have seen. And even after this event in his life, Peter still liked to argue . . . One afternoon in Joppa, Peter goes up onto a roof (the flat Middle-Eastern kind!) to pray (Acts 10:9–23). But, as usually happens, he starts to feel hungry, smelling all the good things that are being prepared for the evening meal down below. He falls into a trance and 'sees' a sheet full of animals designated unclean by Jewish law being lowered before him. It is God inviting him to a meal: 'Get up, Peter. Kill and eat.'

Good kosher Peter has a crisis of conscience, and this makes him inclined to argue: 'Surely not, Lord! I have never eaten anything impure or unclean.' God's answer is enlightening: 'Do not call anything impure that God has made clean.'

The specific context of this event is the issue of calling the Gentiles into the kingdom, but the principle is illuminating. If God's verdict on us is that we are clean, then that's that. Silence in court. The Judge has spoken. We don't have to cower in God's presence, waiting for the blow to fall. Instead, we can run into the arms of a Father who wills us to be bold enough to come to him.

> You are already clean because of the word I have spoken to you. (John 15:3)

> How much more, then, will the blood of Christ, who through the eternal Spirit offered himself unblemished to God, cleanse our consciences from acts that lead to death, so that we may serve the living God! (Heb. 9:14)

> Let us draw near to God with a sincere heart in full assurance of faith, having our hearts sprinkled to cleanse us from a guilty conscience . . . (Heb. 10:22)

> If we confess our sins, he is faithful and just and will forgive us our sins and purify us from all unrighteousness. (1 John 1:9)

God's forgiveness isn't some emotional whim: rather, it is based on Christ's cancellation of our debt of sin on the cross. Under Roman law, when his trial was over, a convicted prisoner would be presented with a

'Certificate of debt.' This certificate would list his specific crimes and the punishment he 'owed' as a result. The prisoner would go to jail, and the certificate would be nailed on his cell door. When the sentence was completed, the jailer would remove the certificate and write the word *tetelestai* – 'It is finished' – on it. Then he would roll up the certificate and hand it to the prisoner as a guarantee that he would never be punished for those crimes again. When Jesus cried from the cross, 'It is finished', he wrote this guarantee across your 'certificate of debt' (Col. 2:13–14).

Look up into the sky. Look left at the distant horizon, where the earth's curve blocks any more of the planet's surface from your sight. Look right to the other extreme. This is how far God has taken our sins away from us (Ps. 103:12). This is his verdict. If we insist on slapping ourselves around for his Name's sake, we had better know that he isn't pleased. Our arguing with him over this is to struggle with his love, which seeks to hush us with the kiss of grace.

His verdict is final.

> God's free grace, which effaces guilt, runs up against the intuition which every man has, that a price must be paid . . . God himself has paid the price once and for all, and the most costly price that could be paid – his own death, in Jesus Christ, on the Cross. The obliteration of our guilt is free for us because God has paid the price.[26]

Try to stop arguing. To do so will require self-discipline. Sometimes when we try to deal with our bad guilt – we attend a meeting or perhaps have someone pray for us – we go home and start all over again. We can easily become distracted back into guilt trips and lose our focus. When we are tempted to remember our darker days, we should bring to mind that moment of God's grace. Jesus had done enough to ensure that Peter would never forget that moment by the beach. He had had an encounter with grace that would stay with him for ever. Maybe, years later, when he was tempted to do a spot of 'walking backwards', the memory of it would help him resist the temptation.

The apostle Paul also learned the secret of remembering grace. He certainly had some regrets about his own personal history. Perhaps there were moments when he thought of the stones pummelling into Stephen's body, the smile on his own face as he held the coats of the executioners and spurred them on with bloodthirsty cries. But when he remembered his sinfulness, he called to mind the fact that 'Christ Jesus came into the world to save sinners – of whom I am the worst. But for that very reason I was shown mercy so that in me, the worst of sinners, Christ Jesus might display his unlimited patience as an example for those who would believe on him and receive eternal life' (1 Tim 1:15–16). As we allow the truth of Scripture to wash and renew our minds, as we accept Jesus' authority over us, we learn to accept his verdict.

So, one last time – stop arguing!

Get on with life

Before the breakfast with Jesus was concluded, Peter was given his marching orders (John 21:17–19), but these were words of recommissioning, not rejection. His new ministry was dawning. He was to cast his net wide as a fisher of men, and the catch would be huge.

Joys, trials and all kinds of adventures lay ahead, fresh battles to be won, history to be made. Jerusalem and the world beckoned. The fireside breakfast was over, but the flames of the Spirit's fire would come. They would flow through him, bringing strange praises to his lips (Acts 2). The warning fire of denial flickered and died. The guilt trip was over; no longer was Peter to wallow around in defeat. There was no time to 'sink out of sight', no time to be paralysed by shame. Leave the denial behind forever, Peter. Get on with life. Stop walking backwards.

And he did.

Chapter 8

Kiss of life

He ran to his son, threw his arms around him and kissed him
(Luke 15:20).

When I began working on this book, I decided not to
take the *Ten-steps to Getting Rid of Bad Guilt, Beginning
with Z* approach. Guilt is a complex issue, and a recipe of
clichés isn't helpful. I do, however, want to draw together some specific points to summarise the snapshots of
guilt we have explored together. I ask you to consider
them in the light of your own situation.

In chapter 1 we discovered that 'walking backwards'
is a popular hobby among Christians. Living in your
past, sweating under the burden of not being good
enough, is something many Bible-believing Christians
do. If you suffer in this way you are not alone: many are
obsessed with feelings of guilt, making the same mental
journey over past mistakes, confused and anxious that
God might be punishing them for their failures. This can
go on for years.

In chapter 2 we looked at the burden of false guilt,
how it weighs us down and blinds us to the fact of our
own spiritual and personal growth. False guilt puts a

mask on the face of God and turns him into a monster. Ultimately, false guilt robs us of joy and life. This kind of guilt is *not* from God: on the contrary, it may destroy us.

In chapter 3 we explored the point that not all guilt is destructive or unhelpful. It's good to feel guilty when we really are. Think about your own experience. Do your guilt feelings stem from actual wrong-doing? If they do, you need to turn away from that wrongdoing and ask God for forgiveness. However, realise that you must sort out the difference between true and false guilt. Your conscience is a helpful but not infallible guide. It is vital to 'programme' your conscience with the truth of Scripture and to balance it with the counsel of wise friends. So ask yourself, are you being convicted or condemned? Does your guilt point to a specific issue that needs to be dealt with (conviction)? Or are you just being overwhelmed by a general sense of failure that nothing and no one can change (condemnation)? Do your guilt feelings offer you a specific way forward? Or do they leave you feeling hopeless and helpless? Do you feel you are being asked to pay for your sins? Or is there a sense that God is offering you his outrageous mercy and forgiveness? Try to sort out the muddle in your mind and heart.

In chapter 4 we discovered the role Satan plays in instigating false guilt. Wake up to the fact that he is your sworn enemy. He is jealous of the freedom you enjoy in God's presence. He wants to confuse you, to accuse you – that is his nature. Don't be surprised that you feel accused, and don't assume that these accusations come from God. Beware the 'house of thoughts' in your mind that Satan has put there. He wants to make God look like a tyrant. He wants to take away your hope and encourage you to run away, a frightened fugitive, from God. Satan goes on and on and on. We need to stand firm in the truth and resist him.

In chapter 5 we explored how false guilt may be generated by negative religion. Is your church a community that preaches grace, love and mercy? Or does it deliver a constant message that everyone is always wrong and you should all just straighten up? Does your church offer relevant teaching to help you live life in the real world? Or is it trapped in a 'ghetto' mentality? Does everyone tend to look the same, act the same, think the same? Are there petty rules that don't seem to have much to do with the Bible? Is your church at ease with joy, fun and laughter?

In chapter 6 we looked at the life of a shame-addict, Peter, and began to explore some of the ways guilt feelings can be resolved. Is the idea that Jesus can see everything about your life a source of encouragement and comfort, or does it fill you with alarm? Are you one of those people who believes the gospel, but who has a sneaky feeling that it might just all be a little too good to be true?

In chapter 7, we continued to look at Peter's life and the way Jesus freed him from guilt. God loves you. He is glad to be around you, even in your painful state of guilt. If there is sin in your past which you regret, then face it once and for all. Get real with Jesus, and get real with the people you know, particularly those you feel you can confide in. Confess your shortcomings and find healing. God is desperate that you leave your guilt behind. He whispers and shouts his message of forgiveness: he loves you and hates your false shame. Surrender. Accept the forgiveness of God. It cannot be earned; it is a mind-boggling gift. Stop arguing with God! Who are you to trash yourself? Who are you to refuse to accept Jesus' ultimate sacrifice – his own life blood – so that you can stop walking backwards? Whether you 'feel' forgiven or not, turn round right now and get on with the rest of your life.

As soon as the telephone rang, I knew that the call was for me and that it wasn't good news. I was right. I had boarded the plane to Belfast with a heavy heart, wanting to be faithful to my preaching engagements but aware that my father was very, very ill. I was so grateful for the quality time we had been able to have together in recent weeks.

I picked up the phone and my fears were confirmed: Dad was dying. I was to cancel everything and rush home immediately, on the next plane. I threw my things into a bag and hurried in the chilly darkness to the airport.

Two hours later, I rushed into Dad's hospital room. He was conscious and, as I took his hand and smoothed his hair, he smiled but said nothing. My dad had been unable to speak for some four years. He loved to talk, had an opinion about everything. But that gift had been stolen from him by a stroke which reduced his speech to meaningless drivel. He knew what he wanted to say, but just couldn't get his brain to make his mouth work. He had faced the frustration and imprisonment of the stroke with bravery.

Now, as I sat at his bedside, I knew that time was short. 'Dad, I'm so glad to see you.' And then, any British reserve overcome by the extremity of life and death, I blurted out, 'Dad, I love you so very much. You do know that, don't you?' He smiled, but then his eyes clouded over. I could see he was struggling to say something important, but the words couldn't come out. However, he had overcome this handicap before. My dad knew how to communicate without words.

Some months earlier, before he had become very ill, I'd been staying overnight at my parents' home. It was the end of the day, and I had already retired to my room. There was a knock at the door. Dad came in and knelt down silently by my bed. He took the blankets and the sheets and tucked me in, just like he'd done thirty-five years earlier when I was his five-year-old. With a kiss on my cheek, brushing away a stray hair on my face, he was gone. I lay there in the dark, aware that here was I, a forty-year-old adult, so used to making decisions and fending for myself and my family, and I had just been tucked in and made warm and secure by my frail father. It felt good.

Now, in the hospital ward, he was going to communicate with me one last time. His eyes cleared, his smile returned and he sat up, reached his hands out to me and cradled my tear-stained face gently in his palms. I will never forget his look, sorrow and joy mingled. He leaned forward and, ever so gently, kissed me on the cheek. Then, still cupping my face in his hands, he looked quickly into my eyes again, as if to say, 'Do you understand? Do you get the message? I love you.'

Again he kissed me, and again the look. And again. And again. Until, finally, knowing that I knew, he settled back down onto his pillow and continued his painful, rasping breathing, fading but satisfied.

Within hours I was to stand, together with my mother, in the now discreetly lit ward (they turn the clinical fluorescent lights out so that you don't have to die in their heartless glare) and we held his hands as he died.

As he breathed his painful last and went to be with God, it felt as if something inside me was ripped out, like a brutal surgery. But, in the few months since his death, this wound has been healing through the knowledge that I was so loved by him. Dad went out of his way to let me know.

I share this most personal moment with you, not as an act of self-indulgent sentimentality, but because I discovered something about the heart of God in the

subdued gloom of that hospital ward. It was a pro-
foundly prophetic moment. Dad had demonstrated
something of God's heart to me that day.

Of course, this illustration only goes so far. There is
nothing frail, weak or inadequate about God and his
ability to communicate. Actually, the frailty and weakness is ours as we struggle to see and hear the unseen
God in a world of loud distractions. Yet how hard he
works to love us and to let us know that we are loved,
kissing us with tokens of grace, trying to help us understand, to fathom the depths of his kindness to us.

Witness the prophetic drama of communion as we
take bread and wine in our hands. We discover a God
who communicates through far more than just the spoken word: using signs and symbols, he nakedly pours
out the depths of his heart in the drama of baptism. As
the convert goes under the water and emerges dripping
and spluttering, we see acted out before us the totality of
new life in Christ in a way that words alone could never
convey. Look at the smiles of those witnessing the baptism. Look at the soaked clothes, the lank hair; the truth
of a new beginning.

Witness Moses who murders a man and tries to hide
his deed by burying his victim in the sand (Exod. 2:12).
But only a day later, he discovers that his cover-up was
in vain – everyone knows what he has done. In shame
and fear he flees to Midian. But God finds him and, forty
years later, he emerges to begin one of the greatest, most
significant tasks in biblical history.

Witness the prophet Hosea, commanded to take a
whore as his bride, so that Israel would be able to see a
daily domestic dramatisation of the faithful love of God
towards a wayward prostitute people (Hos. 1:2).

Witness Paul, or rather Saul, persecutor of the Early
Church. Christians flee from him in terror as, with

ruthless zeal, he harries them mercilessly, seeking to stamp out this upstart faith once and for all. But Jesus grabs him and throws him to the ground on the road to Damascus (Acts 9:1–6). He emerges from the encounter as one of Jesus' most passionate servants.

Witness King David, who spends a thousand nights remembering that moment of passion with Bathsheba and the appalling crime he committed afterwards . . . (2 Sam. 11:2–17).

Witness most of all Jesus the Son of God, skewered crudely yet willingly to a cruel cross. Nothing discreet abut his nakedness. Nothing stage-managed about his last cries. This was no quiet hint, no subtle inference. This was a sob of love from heaven, a frantic God desperate to let an orphan world know that there is love, grace and meaning in the midst of our futility. God shouts and acts, he does everything possible to let us know we are loved and forgiven.

I can still feel Dad's worn hands gentle on my cheeks. I can still see his smile, telling me I was loved, asking if I understood just how much. I let Dad love me. I was powerless in that moment, my adult sophistication sent packing by grace. 'If you, then, though you are evil, know how to give good gifts to your children, how much more will your Father in heaven give good gifts to those who ask him!' (Matt. 7:11).

There may not be physical hands to touch you or a warm kiss to brush your cheeks, but know this: you *are* loved. The nails through his hands shout it: do not doubt it. Jesus died to take that heavy load off your back, to set you free from the moments in the past you regret and which, if you could, you would probably love to go back in time and undo – things you have done that you are ashamed of, words you have said that bruise. But though there is no time machine, you don't need one.

There is a cross, there is a Christ who died, who was raised, who longs to take the eclipse of guilt away, so that you can enjoy the warm sunshine of his love. The long, limping struggle to walk backwards will finally come to an end.

Let him love you.

Endnotes

[1] Smedes, L., *Shame and Grace: Healing the Shame We Don't Deserve* (London: SPCK, 1993), p. 5.

[2] *Shame and Grace*, p. 42.

[3] *Shame and Grace*, p. 18.

[4] *Shame and Grace*, p. 17.

[5] Dobson, J., *Emotions: Can You Trust Them?* (Ventura, CA: Regal Books, 1980), p. 17.

[6] Dyer, W., *Your Erroneous Zones* (New York: Funk & Wagnalls, 1976), pp. 90–91.

[7] Landers, A., *The Ann Landers Encyclopaedia* (New York: Doubleday, 1978), pp. 514–517.

[8] MacArthur, J., *The Vanishing Conscience: Drawing the Line in a No-faith, Guilt-free World* (Nashville: Word Pub., 1994), p. 168.

[9] Narramore, B., and Bill Counts, *Freedom From Guilt* (Capitol Heights, MD: Vision House, 1974), p. 36.

[10] Wechsler, H., *What's So Bad About Guilt?* (New York: Simon & Schuster, 1990).

[11] Phillips, J.B., *Your God Is Too Small* (London: Macmillan, 1987), pp. 15–16.

[12] Phillips, *Your God Is Too Small*.

[13] Dobson, J., *Emotions: Can You Trust Them?* (Ventura, CA: Regal Books, 1980).

14 Permission sought, but copyright ownership could not be traced.

15 The world *skandalon* is used to describe the good news of the gospel of Christ. It's so good, it's scandalous, an affront to human pride.

16 Raviers, A., *A Do-it-at-home Retreat: The Spiritual Exercises of St. Ignatius Loyola* (San Francisco: Ignatius Press, 1989), p. 231.

17 Wechsler, H., *What's So Bad About Guilt?* (New York: Simon & Schuster, 1990).

18 Sandra, in *Good Guilt, Bad Guilt*, Becca Cowan Johnson (Nottingham: IVP, 1996), p. 26.

19 Wiersbe, W., *The Strategy of Satan* (Carol Stream, IL: Tyndale House, 1979), p. 87.

20 Colbert, Dr T.C., *Why Do I Feel So Guilty When I've Done Nothing Wrong?* (Nashville: Nelson, 1993), p. 16.

21 Swindoll, C., *Grace Awakening* (Nashville: Word Publishing, 1990).

22 Sloat, D., *The Dangers of Growing Up in a Christian Home* (Nashville: Thomas Nelson, 1986), pp. 92, 94.

23 Bonhoeffer, D., *Life Together* (New York: Harper & Row, 1962), p. 185.

24 Bakker, J., *I Was Wrong* (Nashville: Thomas Nelson, 1996).

25 White, J., *Putting the Soul Back Into Psychology* (Downers Grove: IVP, 1987), pp. 33–36.

26 Tournier, P., *Guilt and Grace* (New York: Harper & Row, 1962), p. 185.